THE WAY OUT

by the same author

THE SECOND IMPERIALIST WAR

FIGHTING FOR PEACE

THE PEOPLE'S FRONT

WHAT IS COMMUNISM?

COMMUNISM IN THE U. S.

EARL BROWDER

The Way Out

NEW YORK

INTERNATIONAL PUBLISHERS

FOREWORD

In these days when the people of the United States are but awakening to the terrible fact that our country has been fully seized from within by the same forces which have reduced so much of Europe, Asia, and Africa to a bloody shambles, and so many great cities to ruins; when the shadows of tyranny, imperialist war, famine, and pestilence reach across the oceans to darken our own shores—it is not too early to raise for most serious study, and for answer in practical terms, the question of "The Way Out."

This is the question most feared by the ruling class, the bourgeoisie, and by its ideologists and statesmen. Indeed, these gentlemen and ladies have already looted the historical armory of the Inquisition to find weapons to combat this question with its inevitable answer.

The story of Galileo, under the Inquisition, has again, as so many times in American history, an immediate significance for us. Let us recall the story. In the early seventeenth century, Galileo, a foremost representative of progressive humanity of his day which was reaching out to understand and master the world, was halted in his progress by the stone wall of Church Dogma and Law, which proclaimed that the earth was flat and immobile, and that all contrary conceptions were heresy, punishable by death. But Galileo became convinced that the earth was round, and that it moved, and that all future progress depended upon the recognition of this truth. When he propounded this new truth, he was seized and imprisoned by the Inquisition, and put on trial, in 1633, in Rome. Found guilty of heresy, Galileo was given the choice between retraction or being burned at the stake. Not being prepared for the latter, Galileo knelt before his inquisitors and solemnly pronounced the retraction: "I abjure, curse, and detest the error and heresy of the motion of the earth." Then as the jailors released their

5

grip, and he rose from his knees, he muttered to himself in an under-
tone: "But the earth does move."

Eventually, through years of struggle and suffering, the Dogma and
the Law were defeated. The Inquisition was overthrown and disappeared, leaving behind only a dishonorable memory. Galileo with his
stubborn insistence upon the truth, even in the moment when to preserve
his life he was forced formally to retract it, became one of the great
legends of all mankind.

In the United States today, there are laws being multiplied everywhere
which make it heresy to utter the only possible answer to the question
of "The Way Out." This book is therefore a "dangerous" one. If the
reader should become convinced that its answer to the question is true,
and if he should publicly proclaim this fact, he may by authority of
laws of the United States and of various states be deprived of employment, public or private; he may be deprived of his right to vote or to
run for public office; he is subject to all sorts of spying, snooping, wire-
tapping, stool-pigeonry, and slander, from which he will have no legal
recourse, and for which his tormentors will be rewarded, some of them
most richly. If he is stubborn about it, he may find himself suddenly
arrested and sent to prison for a greater or lesser term of years, on the
most sophistical pretexts, such as the case of Oscar Wheeler of West
Virginia, sentenced to fifteen years for gathering signatures to put his
candidacy for the governorship on the ballot.

Yes, it is dangerous to search for "The Way Out," to think any
thought not already blessed by the King and Queen, or one of their
children, or a High Priest. It is especially dangerous to read this book,
unless one is prepared to repeat after Galileo: "I abjure, curse, and detest
the error and the heresy of 'The Way Out' and of all Communist ideas."

It must be admitted that millions of Americans today, like Galileo,
find discretion the better part of valor, so far as their public utterances
and professions are immediately concerned. While seeing ever more the
forbidden truth, they obediently vote for the laws placed before them,
they vote for resolutions condemning Communism and everything it
stands for, they kneel before their Inquisition. But in the very moment
while they recant the "heresy," like Galileo they stubbornly murmur
to themselves: "But the earth does move."

Unlike Galileo's time, today's problem does not present itself entirely
as that of the isolated individual against the all-powerful Inquisition.

Today truth has powerful and growing organizations fighting for its recognition. Above all, today we have a Communist Party which, day in and day out, month after month and year after year, never tiring, never compromising, never wavering, spreads the truth and organizes the seekers for truth, organizes the masses of the people, for "The Way Out."

This book is part of the Communist Party's answer to the Modern Inquisition, that "the earth does move." Unlike Galileo, and his modern prototypes, we refuse to recant and we shout the truth. And we do this in full confidence that the millions of American Galileos who at this moment only mutter the truth under their breath will soon be shouting it aloud with us.

EARL BROWDER

February 26, 1941.

CONTENTS

PART ONE

THE ROAD TO PEACE

I. THE PEOPLE'S ROAD TO PEACE

1. Introduction

THE imperialist war for the redivision of the world is engulfing country after country. The more each imperialist gang of bandits needs a military decision to forestall its own inner collapse, the more desperately does each side call up its reserves, strike out on new adventures, cast the lives and treasures of new millions of men, women and children into the balance. Complete disaster is being inflicted upon nation after nation. And already the American bourgeoisie assumes, as a closed question, that this country is committed to one side of the imperialist rivalry, to the Allied camp, for good or evil, and to question the decision is already a form of treason. In the face of a popular will to keep out of the war, estimated at 96 per cent, the Roosevelt Administration, backed by the united economic royalists and their agents, is taking the country step by step into the war with a speed unexampled in all history, and with a boldness and cynicism that are quite breath-taking, worthy of Hitler himself.

War policy determines everything else. The American bourgeoisie cannot move toward entering the unpopular and imperialist war without, at the same time, making war against the living standards and civil rights of the masses at home, making war against the labor movement, wiping out progressive social legislation, and establishing a more brutal dictatorship of monopoly-capital over the daily life of the country. This domestic side of the war policy of the American bourgeoisie is unfolding itself with equal speed.

The United States and Italy are the only remaining capitalist great powers that have not entered the war as belligerents. Mussolini openly repudiated the concept of "neutrality" from the beginning, and proclaimed Italy as "non-belligerent," which means merely awaiting the most favorable moment to enter as a belligerent. Roosevelt solemnly pledged the United States to a firm neutrality, but used this declaration only the more easily to undermine the anti-war stand of the people. The United States is "sliding" into the war; its position already so closely approximates Mussolini's that the Foreign Minister of Argentina has proposed that the Americas, recognizing reality, shall adopt the Mussolinian formula.

Only one really neutral great power remains in the world, the Union of Soviet Socialist Republics. Firmly repulsing all efforts to drag her into the war on one or the other side, defeating all efforts to switch the war into a general capitalist assault against her rising and victorious socialist system, damming back the war-tide from her most immediate small neighbors, helping the weak nations in their fight for peace and national independence, encouraging the peace forces of all the world—the Soviet Union stands forth as the great stronghold and beacon light of the interests of the working class and the common people of all lands, their hope, their inspiration, and their protection.

The masses of all countries are identifying those who share responsibility for this bloody shambles into which the world has been thrown. They find the responsible ones at the head of all imperialist governments without exception. They are preparing the people's justice for all the guilty ones.

These are the main and decisive features of the national and international situation, which the workers and toiling people of the United States face, as we enter the period of the 1940 Presidential elections.

2. The Imperialist War as the Deepest Crisis of the Capitalist World System

THE present imperialist war is not a *repetition* of the imperialist World War of 1914-18, but is its *continuation*. It is the same in

principle, in that it is the expression of the most profound contradictions of the capitalist system of society (in its imperialist stage
of the dominance of monopoly capital); it is different, inasmuch as
it occurs *after* the last World War with all its consequences, in a
period of more profound crisis, with the forces of world capitalism
much weaker, with the revolutionary anti-capitalist forces much
stronger and more mature, and above all with the existence of the
powerful Soviet Union, a decisive and irrevocable break in the
world system of capitalism. The present war is thus a deeper crisis,
the deepest crisis of the capitalist world.

Tracing back the causes of the present imperialist holocaust, one
is led directly and inevitably, even without the aid of the Marxist-
Leninist theoretical analysis of capitalism, to the worldwide economic crisis that began in 1929, as the starting point of the
immediate chain of events that culminated in the war. Even the
most vulgar bourgeois theoreticians are forced to recognize this
obvious fact, although they try to forget it, and above all to obscure
its significance. But its meaning is inescapable, and already pene-
trates the consciousness of millions of workers in the capitalist
countries; namely, that the seeds of this war are inherent in the
very nature of the capitalist mode of production, and therefore in
the social and political superstructure erected upon that foundation.
Capitalism is itself the general underlying cause of the war.

This conclusion is further driven home when we note that the
war originates as a "family quarrel" between the ruling groups of
the *most powerful* capitalist nations. It is not the "backward"
countries which are forcing war upon the most "advanced," but, on
the contrary, precisely those highest developed in the capitalist sense
which are dragging the less developed one by one into the war.
These ruling groups are closely related to each other. That the
United States, the strongest capitalist country, was not a belligerent
from the first days is due to special historical circumstances, and
does not change the general picture in this respect; and the speed
with which the American bourgeoisie is moving into the very
heart of the war serves to emphasize the inherent drive toward war

that comes from the fundamental nature of the capitalist system. The imperialist war is the violent culmination of the rivalries within the "family" of the international bourgeoisie; in no way does it arise from any inherent contradiction between the peoples involved. The war proves that the common interests of the peoples cannot find organized expression through the capitalist mode of production and the state forms erected upon that basis.

The imperialist character of the present war is even more complete and emphatic than that of 1914-18. Monopoly capital, finance capital, whose dominance in the most powerful countries determines the whole character of modern imperialism, has risen to new heights of power within the various countries, since the last war. The concentration and centralization of capital have proceeded apace, and the great trusts, combines, cartels, and banking syndicates have a much broader and deeper grip upon the economy of each capitalist country. Therefore this war begins as a "total" war on both sides, to a degree even higher than that of the last war after four years of its development.

The uneven development of capitalism, that decisive law of the imperialist stage, discovered by Lenin, is revealed most sharply in this current imperialist war. The disproportion between the real relation of force among the imperialist powers, on the one hand, and the distribution of territories among them, on the other hand, is something which the capitalist nations have no means of adjusting except by the arbitrament of war. The more extreme this disproportion, the more violent is the adjustment. This is the reality hidden behind the distinction between "the have and the have-not nations," which refers not to oppressor and oppressed nations, but to the relationship between military power and possessions. Those governments which complain of being "have-nots" merely mean they have not as much territory as they think they could seize by their military power.

Only the U.S.S.R. stands entirely outside the crisis of capitalism which is the basis of the war. Far from suffering an economic crisis which since 1929 has racked the capitalist world, the Soviet Union, on the contrary, has won through to the greatest prosperity. It has multiplied its national production by more than ten times, over one thousand per cent; and while its position in a hostile capitalist world has forced it to divert an ever-larger amount to defense purposes, its growth in production is so great that, even so, and with an unprecedented proportion going to investment in new means of production, the Soviet Union has still been able to raise the standard of living of all its citizens manyfold. That is the solid material foundation for the peace policy of the Soviet Union, as well as for its ability to maintain its peaceful position against all hostile forces.

How the Capitalist Powers All Helped Prepare the War

Great Britain, France and the United States proclaimed themselves the most completely devoted friends of peace. Together with the smaller countries under their leadership, these powers were possessed, until the last two years, of ample positions and resources to guarantee against any disturbance of world peace. They had the League of Nations, dedicated to that purpose; and if the United States stood aloof from the League, this was more than compensated by the fact that the Soviet Union joined the League, and was most insistent that its proclaimed peace functions be realized. How could it come to pass, therefore, that in a few short years the overwhelming preponderance of power in the hands of these "friends of peace" could be dissipated so much that the rising militarism of Hitler could challenge them in this war with any hopes of success? Why could not the possessors of overwhelming power so use it as to organize peace? How could German imperialism, defeated, prostrate and helpless after the last war, stage such a spectacular comeback in such a short time?

The answer is to be found in two main factors: First, the contradictions and antagonisms among the victors in the last war flared up with new intensity when Germany was defeated, and among the leading powers themselves effectively prevented any common world policy; peace was not the first, but the last, consideration among them. Secondly, the fear of the working class, of the socialist revolution, and especially hatred of the Soviet Union which emerged from the last World War, was so deep and overwhelming within the bourgeoisie, the ruling classes of the whole world, that it led them into fatal miscalculations, into policies which went bankrupt under the test of reality. Bourgeois society, as we look back at it since the World War, presents a most dismal picture of decay, not only economic decay, not only moral decay, but even more completely, if that is possible, intellectual decay. In the whole bourgeois world since the World War, there is not one example of an outstanding statesman, not to speak of a country, which pursued a consistent and long-sighted policy even for the preservation of the bourgeois world, which in their eyes is "the preservation of civilization."

France built her system of hegemony over Europe only to find Great Britain facing her full of jealousy and suspicion, determined to rebuild as quickly as possible a new "balance of power" to replace that destroyed by the World War. The post-war world was a chaos of rivalries, antagonisms, and contradictions.

The phase of "creeping war," which opened the new period of wars and revolutions, began when Japan struck at China in 1931 with the seizure of Manchuria. This was also a heavy blow against the United States, which confidently moved for international support in bringing Japan to heel. But the conference of the signatories of the Nine-Power Pact came to nothing, because Great Britain could not be committed to any action. The United States suspected Great Britain of wanting her to go to war with Japan then, with Britain standing on the sidelines to pick up the pieces, and was certain that the British had double-crossed her.

Hitler, who had come to power with the aid of British and German capital, marched into the demilitarized Rhineland, and announced its forthcoming fortification, but Britain, France, and the League of Nations merely scolded for a moment and were silent. In fact, relations between Britain and France were quite strained, for the French with justice accused the British of encouraging the Rhineland coup, and of playing off both Hitler and Mussolini against them, in order to restore the old game of balance of power on the Continent, which French hegemony had abolished for a time to the discomfiture of Britain. Then Mussolini struck in Ethiopia, and the British Tories, after winning an election on the issue of "collective security," promptly proceeded, in partnership with the French, to sell the Ethiopians down the river. Mussolini and Hitler launched the fascist rebellion of the Spanish Army, and sent their forces in to help strangle the Spanish Republic; Britain and France, supported by the United States, responded by the elaborate farce of the "non-intervention committee" which blockaded the Republic, and these "democracies" publicly rejoiced when Butcher Franco was finally enthroned in power.

Hitler marched into Austria and turned it into a German province, but Britain and France remained silent. Japan invaded China in a bloody, furious war of destruction and made a ferocious assault upon British interests (incidentally machine-gunning the British Ambassador to China), but the U.S.A., Britain and France only mumbled a few words of formal protest, and the U.S.A. continued to furnish Japan with the largest part of the raw materials and machinery required for her war.

Finally, in September, 1938, Chamberlain and Daladier flew to Munich, in order to lay at Hitler's feet the bound and helpless body of Czechoslovakia. *By the Munich Pact, however, the British and French ruling classes had built up Hitler's regime in Germany so far, had surrendered so many strategic points, had so thoroughly destroyed their own moral standing by open complicity with Hitler's crimes, that it was already an open question as to which side was the strongest and, therefore, according to the rules of imperialism, entitled to rule the world. The Frankenstein built up over several years had escaped from the control of its makers.*

It is interesting and instructive at this moment when German arms, having conquered Norway, Denmark, Holland, Belgium, and Luxembourg, are penetrating France so quickly that both London and Paris are threatened, to recall again the long line of events in which the British and French, usually with the acquiescence or assistance of the United States, themselves deliberately and of their own choice broke down and dismantled their whole post-war system of defenses against such a development.

How can such a course be explained, except as inconceivable stupidity or deliberate suicide? Yet we know the men responsible for it are very clever men—indeed; perhaps their trouble was that they were too clever by far. These hard-bitten leaders of the bourgeoisie have no suicidal manias—they may plan death for tens of millions of the people, but never for themselves. How then is it possible to understand their course?

There is but one explanation. The British ruling class had collaborated with their German class brothers in bringing Hitler to power in Germany in order to crush the threatening German socialist revolution, to smash the German Bolsheviks. They were delighted with his performance, and encouraged German rearmament for the purpose of smashing the Soviet Union, which Hitler had long boasted was his chief aim. For this the British and French bourgeoisie were actually happy to see Hitler building an army and piling up armaments. For this they were ready to make most serious concessions to Hitler's axis partners, Japan and Italy, sacrificing China and Ethiopia. For this they gave Mussolini and Hitler a free hand in Spain, to test out those engines of destruction which should later be thrown against the Soviet Union. For this they agreed to allow Hitler to guarantee his "rear" through the fortification of the Rhineland. For this they sacrificed Austria and Czechoslovakia, with untold armaments and treasure. For this they dishonored and emasculated the League of Nations. For this they betrayed their own most solemn obligations and turned them into a mockery before all men. For this they delivered their own fate into the hands of Hitler.

The British and French bourgeoisie had adopted Hitler as their savior with a faith as blind and unquestioning as that of his most ignorant German dupe. Systematically they thereby taught Hitler to despise them, to consider them as fit only for browbeating, blackmail, and if need be, for subjugation. For a chemically-pure example of this fawning British attitude toward Hitler, one need only turn to the pages of the naïve and self-revealing book of Sir Neville Henderson, British Ambassador to Berlin from 1937 up to September, 1939, in which he explains the "Failure of a Mission." Or to Lord Lloyd's booklet, *The British Case,* which is blessed with a preface by Lord Halifax, British Foreign Minister. There is only one "crime" which they are not prepared to forgive Hitler, and that one is his renunciation of the anti-Soviet war. Yes, they were entirely too clever, these great statesmen of British and French monopoly capital, and overreached themselves. In the doing of which they incidentally brought disaster to the peoples of the world, and now to their own lands.

Meanwhile, the Soviet Union was talking quite a different language. Soviet defenses more than matched Hitler's armaments. Hitler's agents were ferreted out of their hiding places, and the country was cleansed of them, along with Japanese and British agents. The Spanish Republic was aided on a scale which, despite its desertion by all the so-called democracies, would have insured its victory had not Blum and Daladier sealed the French border, at crucial moments, to stop the transit of Soviet arms and munitions, and permitted German planes to pass over France into Spain. The Chinese Republic was enabled, by Soviet aid, to resist over years the Japanese *blitzkrieg* conducted with American materials. The Soviet Union never lost an opportunity to urge the implementation of international pledges of collective security. Communists all over the world helped build the anti-fascist People's Front, despite all the betrayals and sabotage from the Second International. Above all, the tremendous achievements of the socialist Soviet economy, multiplying its national income tenfold, and the new Stalinist Constitution of the Soviet Union, made the socialist one-sixth of the world an impregnable fortress. *Facing the vigilant great Soviet Power to the East, and the rotten imperialisms to the West, Hitler disclosed after Munich that he was more inclined to finish up with his imperialist rivals, to revise his original schedule of world con-*

quest, following his well-established tactic of hitting first at the
softest and weakest points.

The British bourgeoisie was thoroughly shaken and frightened
by Hitler's defiant attitude toward it after Munich, especially
when in March, 1939, Hitler marched into Prague, and with the
collaboration of fascist Poland wiped out the remnants of Czechoslovakia. But these British rulers, with the agreement of the French
(and it now appears also of Roosevelt), committed the unbelievable
stupidity of sticking tight to their original grand strategy. They
changed nothing but some details of carrying it through. They still
gambled everything, everything, upon bringing about a war between Germany and the Soviet Union. Hitler was raising his price;
very well, he should get it and more. Not only was Poland to
remain completely defenseless, as a pledge of British "good inten-
tions" toward Hitler, but a "loan" of a billion dollars and a German-
British alliance was dangled before Berlin, on the sole condition
that all moves should be worked out jointly and not by Hitler's
sole decision. To enhance the attractiveness of these offers, Hitler
was to be threatened with the alternative of war. But the threat of
war would have little weight, especially after Munich, unless it was
a threat of war from both East and West. But war from the East
was impossible without the Soviet Union and its Red Army to
conduct it. No one, least of all Hitler, would take such a threat
seriously, unless the weight of the Soviet Union was also behind it.
Therefore, in May the British and French opened conversations
with Moscow for that purpose. Those conversations dragged on
into August.

The British-French negotiators convinced the Soviet Union that
their proposals were not seriously directed to the establishment of
a peace front, but, on the contrary, were designed only to foment a
German-Soviet war under the worst possible conditions for the
Soviet Union. The following incontestable facts were sufficient to
establish this:

(1) In contrast to Chamberlain's airplane flights to Berchtes-
gaden, Godesberg, and Munich, to negotiate directly with Hitler, for

the Moscow negotiations were sent only subordinate officials, practically clerks, and these without any defined powers at all, and even
without any formal credentials.

(2) Their proposals, in essence, were to the effect that in case
Britain could not come to terms with Hitler, then the Soviet Union
should consider itself at war with Germany, but should have no
voice in negotiating those terms, and no rights of action in the
Baltic territories or Poland, even when at war with Germany.

(3) Poland, Britain's vassal, meanwhile stood pat on the position
described recently by General Haller, on the occasion of visiting
Roosevelt, as one of confidence in Hitler and hostility toward the
Soviet Union, an undefended frontier with Germany and no mobi-
lization, but huge fortifications fully manned on the Soviet frontier.

(4) The Baltic States, with British approval, absolutely refused
to discuss any measures for their own and the Soviet Union's defenses in such a war with Germany, while Finland was receiving,
in the very months of the negotiations, forty million dollars' worth
of planes and munitions to supplement the Mannerheim line less
than twenty miles from Leningrad, a line built under British
direction.

These basic factors proved beyond all doubt that the British and
French rulers were merely engaging in a maneuver to bring pressure
upon Hitler to return to his original line of march against the
Soviet Union, and that they had not the slightest intention of negotiating a serious peace front that included the Soviet Union upon a
basis of equality.

At the same time the Germans came to Moscow with the offer of
a far-reaching Pact of Non-Aggression, on the lines which the
Soviet Union had always held out to all nations. Since the Soviet
Union, if not itself attacked, had not the slightest reason to attack
Germany, and since there was no prospect whatever for a real
peace front, this offer was entirely acceptable. It withdrew Eastern
Europe from the immediate threat of becoming the main battle-
ground of the impending imperialist world conflict. It helped dis-
pel the cloud of illusion and falsification that enveloped the world,

reveal the true relation of forces and issues, and give another opportunity to the peace forces of the world to halt the war-makers. It enabled the Soviet Union to perfect its Western defense lines, the weaknesses of which the capitalist world had been boastfully discussing for years. The Soviet-German Non-Aggression Pact, signed on August 23, 1939, knocked into a pile of ruins the whole grand strategy of the camp of Chamberlain-Daladier-Second International built on the fixed idea of using Hitler Germany to destroy the Soviet Union.

With the desperation of gamblers playing a "sure thing system" at roulette, the British-French rulers with their Social-Democratic accomplices (and as we now know, the complicity of the Roosevelt Administration) had doubled and redoubled their stakes. They gambled away the independence of nations and their own honor. They staked the most precious interests of their own peoples. They played with the peace of the world, with the lives of tens of millions of helpless and unknowing people. They gambled—and they lost.

A storm of hysterical rage swept over the bourgeoisie and their hangers-on of the Second International (with its Trotskyite and Lovestoneite appendages), against the Soviet Union, for daring to sign a Pact of Non-Aggression with Germany without their permission. This storm was by no means least violent in the United States, significantly enough, showing how deep in the conspiracy had been our American ruling class. The very men and parties which had most loudly praised the Munich Pact less than a year before—remember, *only* the Communists fought and voted against Munich—now led a most ferocious denunciation of the Soviet-German Non-Aggression Pact as—of all things—"another Munich"! The very men and parties who had been publicly praying for the success of Chamberlain's efforts to secure an agreement with Hitler on.how to divide up the world—these were the ones to denounce the Soviet-German agreement merely not to go to war with one another. The depth of this hysteria among the bourgeoisie and their "Socialist" lackeys is a measure of the completeness of the bankruptcy of imperialist policy thereby revealed. The gamblers could not accept the fact that they had lost.

Trying to Swap the "Wrong War" for the "Right War"— First Stage of the Second Imperialist Slaughter

In the first days of September the British Government, and after it the French, declared war against the Frankenstein of their own creation, because it had escaped from their control and renounced its original mission. But it was with the outspoken cry that came sincerely from their imperialist hearts that this was the "wrong war," which should be exchanged as quickly as possible for the "right war," for the war they had been conspiring so many years to bring about. Their slogan, "Swap the wrong war for the right war," is the key to an understanding of the whole course of war from September to March of this year, the period of the "phony war." It meant that the British-French rulers were still, incredible as it seems that such stupidity could be possible, bullheadedly persisting on the path of the bankrupt and shattered grand strategy of the anti-Soviet war. Having failed to bribe and persuade Hitler to go through with it, they now undertook to force him to do so. That goal determined the whole form and spirit of the first stage of the war. Its disastrous consequences for the Allies are only now becoming apparent, in the second stage of the war. Instead of correcting the fundamental error which had brought them to catastrophe, they intensified it, and thereby redoubled its terrible consequences. And in this stage, the Roosevelt Administration from secret complicity emerged into open and active partnership.

Ostensibly the war began over Poland. That was only a convenient pretext, however, as uncontested facts amply prove. Britain had no more intention of defending Poland than she had previously had of defending Austria, Spain, or Czechoslovakia. The British Government did not even sign its *paper guarantee* of Poland until the last days of August, when the war had already been decided upon; it had negotiated an insignificant loan to Poland, but even that fell through, because they could not agree how it should be spent. The Polish army was never fully mobilized, and not even a trench was dug on its German borders, although its Soviet frontier bristled with modern fortifications. The Polish Government was itself fresh from the feast, together with Hitler, on the body of Czechoslovakia. It had not conceived of the idea, nor had its British mentors, of resisting Hitler in any serious way. Chamberlain had sent a note to Hitler, on August 28, offering him the same kind of settlement of the Polish issues that he had already provided in the case of Czechoslovakia. The sole issue was narrowed down to whether Hitler should take what he wanted by force or whether he should receive it from the hands of Chamberlain as a gift. In this issue was concealed the true matter of dispute, which was not Poland, but whether Hitler accepted Chamberlain as an equal partner in the redivision of the world.

The Polish Government, with most of the generals of its army, broke and fled the country in the first weeks of the German onslaught; their only efficient preparations had been to pack their treasures, money, jewelry, and so on, for a hasty flight to London and Paris.

With the collapse and flight of the Polish Government, the Soviet Red Army occupied Western Ukraine and Western Byelo-Russia, rescuing some thirteen million inhabitants, including more than two million Jews, immediately incorporating them with full equality in the autonomous Soviet Republics, giving them land and reorganizing their economic life. The western bourgeoisie (including the American and especially the Jewish-American) was more indignant against this rescue by the Red Army than they were against Hitler; rescue missions, they thought, were only permissible when undertaken by commission of His Majesty the King and Emperor of the British Empire, through his faithful servant, Neville Chamberlain.

The little Baltic states of Esthonia, Latvia and Lithuania, which with Poland had been Britain's pawns in the so-called "peace front" negotiations with the Soviet Union, and provided Britain with its desired "insuperable obstacles" to meeting Soviet views, now that they were released from the threat of British interference, underwent a sudden and profound change of heart. They quickly signed mutual defense pacts with the Soviet Union, providing for Soviet naval and military outposts on the Baltic, and for the rescue of their economies from collapse by close trade relations with the Soviet Union. Lithuania received her ancient capital, Vilna, seized by Poland in 1920, as a free gift from the Soviet Union. All three countries have been profuse in their praise of how the Soviet Union has carried out these agreements. But Britain, France and the United States had exerted every effort to prevent these agreements from being signed.

Then negotiations opened between Finland and the Soviet Union. The Soviet Union asked that the Finnish frontier close to Leningrad be moved back, for a lease on Hangoe Peninsula for a naval base to protect the Gulf of Finland, for some small readjustments in the north to protect Murmansk; and offered Finland compensating territorial adjustments of tenfold area and economic value, together with favorable economic relations and a mutual defense pact. There cannot be the slightest doubt that a quick and peaceful settlement would have been made, but for the intervention of Allied and American influence. President Roosevelt made a public intervention based upon the assumption that the Soviet proposals must be rejected, and placing his influence in support of such a decision, presumably assuming responsibility for the consequences. Mannerheim, Ryti and Tanner felt cocky, indeed; did they not have the most powerful forces of the world in their support? They went so far as to permit themselves the luxury of provocative incidents violating the Soviet frontier. Again, the imperialist forces had over-reached themselves. The Red Army marched into Finland.

That was the moment when the bourgeoisie, and particularly the American bourgeoisie, together with all their "Socialist" and "labor" lickspittles, opened up their hearts and minds for the whole world to see what was really there. With one voice they all shouted that no sacrifice was too great if only it would preserve the Mannerheim Line at the throat of Leningrad. "The war in Finland" took precedence over the war with Germany, which, especially in America, found itself relegated to the back pages of the newspapers. *The great empires of the world were supposedly locked in a life-and-death struggle, but the one single spot where the Allies, plus the United States, plus Italy, were willing to assume the military offensive was on the Mannerheim Line against the Soviet Union!* The Roosevelt Administration rushed huge loans to Mannerheim; Herbert Hoover opened up public subscriptions for arms and supplies; the newspapers presented Mannerheim with miraculous military victories gratis every day; the public test of true Americanism became a pledge of allegiance to the Mannerheim-Ryti-Tanner Finnish government, to refuse which was considered substantially treasonable! What a revelation that was of the true desires and thoughts of the bourgeoisie! Here at last was the "right war" which they were ready to move heaven and earth to substitute for the "wrong war" with Hitler! Let us never forget this revelation of the true mind and heart of the bourgeoisie, of the ruling classes, which has not changed one iota, although with the ebb and flow of military fortunes it is often covered with sweet words and gestures, and a pretense of a new "friendliness" toward the Soviet Union.

During the period of hostilities in Finland, Allied-American grand strategy was reconstructed in terms of holding tight on the Western front, while active military measures were assigned to the "Northern front" and the "Southeastern front," both of them capable of being directed against Germany or the Soviet Union, or both, with equal facility. The plan was to move simultaneously on both fronts in May, in a pincers movement, which, backed by the blockade and a solid Western front, would "bring Hitler to his senses" and a quick peace, followed by a concerted drive against the Soviet Union, the "'right war" at last. The world-shaking achievements of the Red Army in smashing the Mannerheim Line, and the Soviet-Finnish peace on March 12, without precedent in the generosity of its terms, again shattered the reconstructed Allied strategy.

While these events were taking place, President Roosevelt made his first ambitious attempt at direct diplomatic intervention to change the course of the war. He sent Sumner Welles on his dramatic tour through Rome, Berlin, Paris and London. According to the best available information Welles carried proposals, already agreed upon with the Vatican, with London and Paris "agreed in principle" (that is, prepared to discuss as a basis of settlement), whereby Italy was to receive Tunis, Corsica, Jibouti, and an equal voice in control of Suez, in return for pressing Hitler to accept a "token" reconstitution of Poland and the status quo in the West, return of German African colonies, and a free hand and practical assistance in the East against the Soviet Union—the whole settlement to be guaranteed by the United States, which would assume the role of "honest broker" between the rivals and policeman of the new "community of nations." Unfortunately for Roosevelt's ambitions, the market price for Mussolini's services had taken a big jump just at the moment Welles started on his trip, and when he arrived in Rome, he found his currency so highly depreciated that it would buy nothing. Mussolini had adopted Lloyd George's famous phrase as his answer—"Too late and too little." Welles returned to Washington a sadder if not a wiser man.

The first phase of the imperialist war came to a close with a situation which, according to former standards, was a military stalemate, and a diplomatic deadlock; with the United States out in the open as the "non-belligerent" ally of Britain and France, corresponding to Italy's position as "non-belligerent" ally of Germany; with feverish preparations on both sides to extend the war to the small countries; and with the Soviet Union, the only truly neutral great power, greatly strengthened and at peace, more than ever the center of attraction of all the peace forces of the world.

Marking the close of the first phase of the war, Prime Minister Neville Chamberlain, speaking to Britain and the world, uttered those historic words: "Hitler has missed the bus!" The next day, the second phase of the war opened with the British mining of Norwegian territorial waters. Within six weeks German troops were within artillery range of British shores.

THE "WRONG WAR" BECOMES THE REAL WAR

Less than two months' engagement of the main imperialist forces in military combat (hardly three weeks if we disregard the Norwegian preliminaries), already promise to exceed all estimates of the deadly and destructive nature of modern warfare between great powers. Despite seven months of "phony" war, that is, war largely confined to economic and diplomatic moves, it now appears that casualty lists, civilian and military, will quickly overtake and surpass those of the last war. It is not possible as yet to make any decisive estimate of the course and consequences of this second phase of the war. A few conclusions are, however, clearly in order:

First, the speed of events clearly is transforming the war into a *world war* on the largest scale with the possibility of the greatest catastrophes. The very concepts of "neutrality" and "national independence" have become meaningless for most of the world, killed by the actions and policies of both belligerent camps. Britain first violated Norwegian neutrality, thus sharing the moral responsibility of Germany; the only difference was that Britain did it first while Germany did it most successfully, thoroughly and effectively. The Allies boldly announced that "neutral rights" would no longer be any barrier to what they considered necessary military measures, just before the Germans acted upon their words by striking through Holland and Belgium. The United States has been poised for entrance into the war by Roosevelt's actions, and especially by his latest declarations, which may any moment receive a powerful push from the Far East, in the dispute over the rubber, tin and oil resources of the Dutch East Indies, with Japan preparing to realize her imperialist "manifest destiny." Rumors of a possible transfer of the seat of the British Empire to Canada serve to emphasize the seriousness of involvement of all the Americas, through the pro-war policies in Washington, and the unbridled grasping for profits of American capital.

Second, the initiative in the war has been definitely seized by the Germans, with all the advantages that accrue therefrom, largely as the result of Allied-American obsession with the aim of "switching the war" against the Soviet Union. The advantage of this initiative has been further emphasized by the revelation that air power has gained over sea power since the last war, as shown not only in the Skagerrak but also on the Norwegian Atlantic Coast, with deadly intimations following for the Mediterranean area. This, however, is not the main reason for the present campaign of panic and pessimism over Allied military prospects, spread among their partisans in America, any more than the situation at the beginning of April justified the Pollyanna optimism of Chamberlain's cheerful chuckles at that time, less than two months ago. The jitters and gloom, spreading from London and Paris, arise more from fear of their own population, disillusioned and disgusted with their ruling classes and rebelling against the indescribable horrors imposed upon them, and against admitted incompetence, if not treason, in high places. Then, also, pessimism at this moment is a form of pressure upon the American bourgeoisie openly to enter the war as a belligerent, in order to offset the moral effect of their setbacks, to offset Mussolini's probable entrance on the other side, and—not least important—to forestall some possible demands the American bourgeoisie might make at the expense of Britain if they have more time to think the matter over. Pessimism over the present situation is thus a not too delicate form of blackmail against Washington and Wall Street, threatening a possible "quick peace" at the expense of American imperial ambitions, since it is no longer feasible to do it at the expense of the Soviet Union.

Third, the perspective of a long war of blockade and attrition, upon which Great Britain was orientated last September as the final guarantee of success, failing all efforts to "switch the war," no longer holds any promise of achieving the larger aims of British imperialism. This is because (a) the blockade is not as effective as it had been supposed; (b) the Empire ties with the Dominions, India and Ireland already reveal dangerous strains which may become very acute under a prolonged war; (c) Japanese and American demands and aspirations, directed to the field of British imperialist interests, become ever more embarrassing, costly and threatening for the future; (d) economic strain and threatening crisis is becoming almost, if not fully, as potent a factor for Britain and France as for Germany and Italy; and finally (e) the working class and toiling masses generally are, from the beginning, almost entirely without enthusiasm for this war, even where they are not yet vocally and actively against it, and the bourgeoisie is becoming acutely conscious of the threat of popular upheavals, leading toward socialist revolutions. The Allied Powers are therefore tending to abandon the perspective of a long war, and want above everything now to bring in the United States as the necessary reserve for a military decision in their favor.

It is on this background that we must evaluate the call ·to war issued by President Roosevelt at the Pan-American Scientific Congress, and his hysterical juggling with flying-time schedules and "fifty thousand planes" when appealing for expansion of the Army and Navy appropriations to three and a half billion dollars. All these things are understandable, they have a definite logic, *only* as preparation for quickly and fully throwing the United States as a belligerent into the imperialist war between Britain and France, and Germany, into military adventures overseas.

The "wrong war" has become the real war. The real war is becoming a world war. The world war is getting set to engulf the United States also—if the American workers and lovers of peace allow this to happen.

◄ THE WAR-GUILT OF THE SECOND INTERNATIONAL

Long ago the working class and democratic masses generally would have halted the war-makers, and made it impossible for them to throw the world into war, but for the fact that they were held back, demoralized, split up, and delivered over to the control of the bourgeoisie by their treacherous misleaders of the parties of the Second International, the so-called "Socialist" and "labor" parties, and the reactionary trade union leadership that follows them.

The parties of the Second International share fully and completely the war-guilt of the imperialist profiteers, in an even more degraded and disgusting form, because they cover themselves with the hypocritical cloak of phrases about "socialism in the future" and "the interests of labor," with the most brazen demagogy. The Attlees and Citrines in England, the Blums and Jouhaux in France, the Norman Thomases, Sidney Hillmans and William Greens in the United States, one and all performed the most indispensable services to the imperialist war-makers, without which they would never have been able or have dared to plunge the world into war.

The case of the Spanish Republic is a key example of this traitorous role of the Second International. If the German armies have swept over the small Western European countries and now hammer at the gates of Paris and London, this is possible *only* because in the spring of 1939 the Mussolini-Hitler-Franco armies were able to take Barcelona and Madrid and finally strangle the Spanish Republic. *If the Spanish Republic had emerged victorious there is not the slightest doubt that this alone would have prevented the outbreak of the Second Imperialist War in 1939.* For over two years, throughout the heroic struggle of Republican Spain, our Party never tired of pointing this out. One thousand American boys—Communists—died in Spain for democracy—to save the peace of the world. The imperialists and all their agents attacked us then. They put every obstacle in the way of the Spanish Republic. To this day, the U. S. Government has failed to recognize and aid the heroic fighters for Spanish democracy and the Spanish refugees in France, who need our support.

Mussolini and Hitler could never have strangled the Spanish Republic without the co-operation of Chamberlain, Daladier and Roosevelt. But Chamberlain & Co. could never have dared to give that co-operation without the support of the whole Second International. Indeed, it was Leon Blum himself, leader of the French Socialist Party and then Premier of France, who took the initiative in formulating and applying the infamous "non-intervention" scheme. It was the leadership of the British Labor Party which restrained and broke up the mass movement in England that demanded help to Spain. It was the Scandinavian Socialist leaders, holding decisive positions in their governments, who, together with the Dutch and Belgian Socialist leaders, and those of Poland and Czechoslovakia, made up the overwhelming majority of the Second International leadership that unhesitatingly upheld this traitorous policy. It was Norman Thomas in the United States who justified his European colleagues, while covering himself with hypocritical lip-service to Spain, and gave to Roosevelt his cynical reply to all protests against the American embargo: "Do you really expect me to go farther than Leon Blum and the Second International?" It was the Second International leadership which conspired with London, Rome and Berlin to deliver the final blow against the Spanish Republic, by opening up the gates of Madrid, through their miserable agents Casado and Besteiro. *Now it is clear that history will record the delivery of Madrid to the fascists as the opening of the flood-gates of the war that today sweeps over all Europe and extends more and more to the rest of the world.*

It was the Second International which prevented the successful building of the People's Front against reaction and war. When the French Socialist masses forced their leaders to enter the Front Populaire, it was Leon Blum who conspired night and day to dissolve it, who never rested until he had shattered this powerful alliance of the people from within. In England it was Attlee and Citrine who forcibly suppressed the People's Front movement, which could long ago have brought down the Chamberlain Government and opened the way to peace. In the United States it was Norman Thomas and the reactionary trade union leaders who took the lead in denunciation of the People's Front and the democratic front for peace, in the most extreme and slanderous terms.

Since the Second Imperialist War is on, it is the Second International in each country which has most shamelessly and unconditionally led the shouting for the most extreme war party. Their only complaint against the war is that it is not yet also a war against the Soviet Union.

The fight for peace, and for defending the economic and political

needs of the workers and toiling masses, can be successful only to
the degree that it meets, exposes, isolates, and defeats all these warmongering agents of imperialism among the people.

ONLY ONE ROAD OF SUCCESSFUL STRUGGLE AGAINST THE WAR

The overwhelming majority of people of every country hate this
war, and want to stop it immediately. The ruling classes of each
warring camp reply: yes, we all want peace, but peace can come
only through victory for our side; therefore the only road to peace
is to sacrifice everything for the war. In the United States, where
96 per cent of the people are against entering the war, the answer
is given that the only way to peace is to enter this war to guarantee
victory to the Allied cause. Thus the agents of the high financiers
and war-profiteers try to turn the very aspirations for peace into the
mightiest engine for war.

Along this road lie only catastrophe, misery, starvation and death
for the peoples of the world. The choice of supporting the "lesser
evil" against the worst evil leads not to peace, but to the sure inflic-
tion of every possible evil upon the masses. Not the victory of one
or another imperialist camp is the road to peace, but the victory of
the people over their war-making rulers in each country is the only
way.

What reason is there to believe that an Allied victory will bring
anything better to the world than a German victory? Britain and
France emerged the victors in 1918, with such tremendous powers
in their hands as had never existed before in the world, not only
the power to dictate the terms of peace to the vanquished, but even
to dictate to their own allies, the United States, Italy and Japan,
not to mention the smaller powers. What did they do with their
power? What kind of Europe and what kind of world did they
produce? If the world is in a bloody mess today, that is the·direct
result of victory for the Allied Powers in 1918. Have the British and
French ruling classes showed any intelligence or morality since
1918 greater than before? On the contrary, they have shown even
less. Have they shown any more ability? On the contrary, they

display nothing but an abyss of incapacity, ineptitude and corruption. Are they any more "democratic"? On the contrary, they have leveled off the so-called democracies with the fascist regimes, so that there is no essential difference between them in their relationship to the masses. There is nothing to choose between the imperialist camps, for any support given to either means the surrender of the whole struggle for peace and a better world.

Only the peoples of the world, led by the working class, can bring peace and a better world, and that only by struggle and victory over *their own* imperialists and reactionaries.

The people of the United States can protect themselves and help the rest of the world only by resisting and defeating all those who want to help one side against the other, which leads finally and inevitably to entering the war; only by fighting against every tendency to spread the war anywhere in the world; only by fighting and defeating the tremendous efforts being made to establish a war regime within the United States even before the entry into the war; only by fighting against and defeating the armaments program which is only a greased chute to catapult this country overnight and against its will into the war.

The only road of successful struggle against the imperialist war is that so sharply and clearly defined in the words of George Dimitroff in *The Struggle Against the Imperialist War*:

First, union of the fighting forces of the working class within each country;

Second, a genuine popular front of the working people, led by the working class;

Third, united action of the proletariat internationally, and its own independent, single international policy of struggle against imperialist war;

Fourth, combination of the struggle of the working people of the capitalist countries with the anti-imperialist movement in the colonial and dependent countries;

Fifth, rallying the working people around the great Land of Socialism, the only state which champions the cause of peace among nations and which defends the vital interests of the working people of the whole world.

This is the only path which can rescue the world from the chaos and destruction of imperialist war. This is the path which we must help the American working class, at the head of the whole people, to find in the most concrete fashion, for our own country.

3. Domestic Reactionary Development Is but the Other Side of the War Policy of the Bourgeoisie

UNDER the slogan of "national unity" the economic royalists and their agents are rallying the entire bourgeoisie against the working class and toiling masses, they are splitting the nation into two camps with a decisiveness that has never before been witnessed. They are making united war against the labor movement, against the living and working standards of the masses, and against popular civil rights. This is the domestic policy which inevitably accompanies an imperialist war policy. President Roosevelt, assuming the leadership of the war party, has thereby also assumed the leadership of domestic reaction. The New Deal chapter of progressive social legislation, always fragmentary and lacking consistency, has now definitely closed.

The Roosevelt regime was inaugurated almost simultaneously with that of Hitler in Germany. Both arose from the same deep and catastrophic economic crisis of the capitalist world system, and the impossibility of finding any way out by "normal" means. *They took different paths,* because the German bourgeoisie had united, with British support, upon the course of open brutal dictatorship to suppress the home population, and intense preparation for foreign wars; whereas the American bourgeoisie split after a short period when it was in doubt which way Roosevelt was moving; the most reactionary section went in the Hitler direction while a "liberal" section rallied the masses to its support for a "liberal experiment" in progressive domestic and foreign policy to meet the crisis. This came to be identified as the "New Deal" and the "Good Neighbor" policies. Both of these are now dead. The Rooseveltism of the New Deal has capitulated to the reactionaries. A new Roosevelt is again bosom friends with that evil old man Garner and his friends. The new Roosevelt course is for America essentially the same direction which Hitler gave for Germany in 1933. Unless it is halted, and a different course charted for our country, it can only have a similarly catastrophic end. In the name of the fight against Hitlerism, the American bourgeoisie boldly strikes out on the path of imitation. Its period of appeasement of the people has ended. Monopoly capital, dominating our society, has in the end no other answer to the questions raised by the crisis and breakdown of its economic system than that given in the past years by its European class brothers. It is the answer of black reaction and war.

But from 1935 up to the outbreak of the imperialist war, a section of the bourgeoisie in a loose sort of coalition with labor, the poorer farmers, the Negroes, the youth, the unemployed, had tried to lead the United States on a different path, the path of social reform and concessions to the masses, with peaceful and conciliatory relations with Latin America and the rest of the world. That was the period of the New Deal, in which the obsolete and disintegrating old party structure had largely dissolved into two new camps—the New Deal and the anti-New Deal—in which American newspapers and the economic royalists were almost as fierce in their hatred of Roosevelt as they are now of the Communists.

How long ago that period seems now! Yet, when we check with the calendar, it was less than a year ago that Roosevelt was accused of being a Red, or at least a "Communist stooge" and an agent of Moscow. It is only somewhat more than a year ago that a solemn Senate Committee gravely demanded to know of Mr. Felix Frankfurter, prominent New Dealer, if he were a member of the Communist Party, and, only upon his equally grave reply that he was not, unanimously confirmed him to life membership in the Supreme Court. Less than a year ago Martin Dies was a deadly enemy of the Administration of which he is today the ideological and political vanguard. Less than a year ago Elliott Roosevelt was publicly panning papa on the radio and boosting papa's most virulent enemy in the Democratic Party; but now papa has won son's endorsement for a third term by uniting with son's employers. It is less than ten months ago in fact; but so much water has run under the bridge in that time that it seems like ten years!

Today, Dorothy Thompson, the unique and inimitable, no longer her usual jump ahead of her political camp, plumps for a third term for Roosevelt on Republican and Democratic tickets with Wendell Willkie as his running-mate! Yes, it is unquestionably the same Dorothy. Only the times have changed, and the alignment of classes, and the bourgeoisie is at war—war among their different governments and war against the working class and toiling masses everywhere!

Today there are eighty-five trade unions of the American Federation of Labor and the Congress of Industrial Organizations indicted under the Sherman Anti-Trust Law, for conspiracy to organize the workers of their industries. Ben Gold, Irving Potash, and a dozen associates of the Fur Workers Union have been sentenced to long prison terms. Twenty-five Teamsters of Local 807, A. F. of L., were convicted and some of them face as high as forty-one years' imprisonment for striving for union conditions and standards. It is the first time in history that any one has ever been sentenced to prison under this law adopted generations ago! And the proceedings are brought by the Roosevelt Administration, heading a united bourgeoisie, with the economic royalists a solidly cheering group in the foreground!

THE WAR POLICY OF REACTION

The great transformation began to develop systematically and swiftly, at the opening of the imperialist war. A simple little reservation to the declaration of American neutrality toward this war—that "we" could not all agree to be "neutral in thought"—started an endless chain of cause and effect that has culminated in a complete regroupment in American politics and brought the U.S.A. to the brink of plunging headlong into the most senseless and destructive war in the history of the world.

"Fifty thousand airplanes" is the slogan which opened up the 1940 Presidential campaign. For what? The answer is a solemn recital of the flying time of various air-schedules into the United States, culminating in the information that from Tampico, Mexico, to Omaha and Kansas City it is only two-and-a-half hours. But Lindbergh was only stating a matter of common knowledge and common sense, whatever his political motive, which is open to question, when he said that no possible enemy could invade the U.S.A. by air, and that the U.S.A. cannot possibly be involved in war except by its own seeking. For what, then, the fifty thousand airplanes and the multiplied billions for the Army and Navy? What, then, is the significance of time schedules of air flights?

Peoples of the twenty Latin American countries will stir uneasily as they reflect that the air time-tables work both ways! The whole world knows of "Wrong-way" Corrigan, and that he is an American national hero! There is no power which could conceivably invade the United States by air, but fifty thousand military airplanes in the U.S. with as many young Corrigans at the controls would be as heavy a sword over the head of Latin America as twelve thousand planes in Germany were for the last years over the head of Europe. The Mexican people must be pondering deeply over the meaning of the mention of Tampico, principal point of distribution of the Mexican oil industry, regarding which the U. S. Government is making demands which the Mexican Government has rejected as infringing upon Mexican integrity and independence. Fifty thousand airplanes become full of meaning for the Latin American peoples, who can now see the three-hundred-mile neutrality zone around the continents as a claim staked out by Yankee imperialism.

What do the fifty thousand airplanes mean to the people of the Pacific, of the Far East? Will the news bring comfort to the four hundred million population of China, who during eight years have suffered much more than Europe all the horrors of modern military invasion, the loss of all their seacoast and large cities, the death of ten millions, with famine for hundreds of millions? No, it will not comfort the Chinese, for they will remember that over the eight years, *the Japanese invaders have carried on only with the supplies furnished by the United States;* that the American conscience has stirred but faintly under the vast profits gained from this trade; that Washington became excited and raised the slogan of fifty thousand planes, in relation to the Far East, only when the future of the rubber, oil, and tin of the Dutch East Indies became an open question. Fifty thousand planes registers an American imperialist claim on the Dutch East Indies.

Greenland, Iceland, the Caribbean islands, these are but the small change in the great gamble of world redivision and world empire into which Roosevelt is leading the American people.

But this bald program of imperialist territorial aggrandizement overseas cannot secure the support of the American people. It is therefore not directly propagandized; it is even indignantly denied. Once the United States is "at war," however, the tail would go with the hide without any possibility of mass criticism. The problem of American imperialism is therefore one of getting the country into war, on any or every pretext, and then their program will have no effective opposition, so they think. How to get into the war, that is the question for our ruling circles.

The United States is already in the war, morally and economically, as a non-belligerent ally of England and France. But the profits from war-trade prove painfully disappointing in volume, and do not keep pace with the losses from the deepening economic crisis. Further, as a non-belligerent it is still impossible to abolish at one stroke all social legislation and trade union safeguards, still impossible to conscript labor, still impossible to implement those beautiful M-day plans, which are the imperialist ideal of heaven on earth. All the irksome problems of "disciplining" unruly labor, of dissolving all "democratic nonsense" in the country, could be so easily cut through with the sword of belligerency, of official entrance into the war!

This, not sympathy with the "democracies" which have turned dictatorships overnight, is the main driving force impelling the

American bourgeoisie into the war. But that sympathy, which exists among the masses together with a hatred of Hitlerism, is counted upon to undermine and overcome the even more clear and emphatic determination among the masses to keep out of this war. This is being strengthened by studied incitations to hysterical fear of the safety of America in the war-torn world. Truly America is in danger, but the bourgeoisie is determined to hide the real danger, which is the danger of being dragged into the war on the Allied side, and the danger of indigenous fascism which springs directly from the economic royalists, from Wall Street. The masses are to be frightened by the specter of invasion from abroad, to accept the yoke of military dictatorship wielded by the economic royalists at home.

This course is all the more acceptable to our American ruling classes, since they also have interests in the European war which they can better advance through a belligerent position. They want Britain to win—not too quickly and not too cheaply, of course! They foresee the British Empire coming out of this war in such a position of dependency upon the American Empire, as formerly the Dutch bore toward Britain, or that to which the French had been reduced in the last few years. The British Empire is an "inheritance" which the American imperialists would therefore not like to see dispersed, although they are not displeased to see Uncle John Bull in poor health. But above all the American ruling class interest in Europe is to do everything possible to check and prevent the outbreak of popular upheavals, which bear the danger of leading directly to the socialist revolution in one or more European countries. Fear of revolutionary upheaval in Europe, and the determination to hold it down by all means is the most powerful general motive driving the American ruling circles toward entrance into the war as a belligerent. Capitalism must be preserved at all costs in Europe if Wall Street is to feel safe in America. That is what the American newspapers and statesmen mean when they say, "In Europe they are fighting our battles for us, and we must help them."

This is the world outlook and program upon which the economic royalists and their political henchmen are united. This is the basis for unity of the bourgeoisie, which takes place so rapidly before our eyes after years of split and the most bitter struggles. It is a unity against labor and the masses at home, against the weaker and dependent countries and for the Allied imperialists as against the German in the war. But it is only a relative unity within which their own quarrels grow more bitter. It is not yet a unity of leadership and method in the struggle for these goals. Our ruling classes have not thoroughly modernized their instruments of rule, and fall into some confusion in driving toward what they want.

From the report to the Eleventh National Convention of the Communist Party of the United States, New York, May 30 to June 2, 1940.

II. A PLATFORM FOR PEACE

THE Communist Party occupies an exceptionally responsible position in the 1940 election. National and international crises press upon our people. The country gropes to find its way in a world which is falling to pieces about us, and the old guides, in whom the nation had placed its faith for seven years, have failed.

In 1937, the man who had the ear of the American people, the President of the United States, spoke the following words:

In our generation, a new idea has come to dominate thought about government—the idea that the resources of the nation can be made to produce a far higher standard of living for the masses if only government is intelligent and energetic in giving the right direction to economic life. That idea ... cannot be thrust aside by those who want to go back to the conditions of ten years ago or even preserve the conditions of today. It puts all forms of government to proof.

When President Roosevelt spoke those words, he voiced the views and hopes of the biggest majority that ever assembled in support of a popular cause in this Western world.

The people still hold to this idea. The Communists supported it then and hold to it now. But the man who spoke those words in 1937 now speaks instead of a multiplied navy and fifty thousand airplanes, a program of armaments that means military adventures in the Dutch East Indies and the Far East, in Latin America and on the blood-soaked fields of Europe. And the shrill howl for armaments blots out the call for "a far higher standard of living for the masses."

The Communist Party gives voice to the deepest convictions of the great majority of the American people, when it calls halt to the deliberate drive into the war, when we cry out to the imperialist war camps: "A plague on both your houses." We speak for the people when we demand a stop to the blood-soaked trade in munitions and instruments of war. We speak for the millions, when we resolve: "The Yanks are *not* coming."

The People's Rights Must Be Preserved

But American economy has been geared to the war market, with immense fortunes accruing to those who already hold immense fortunes, and who dream of realizing their dictatorship through the M-Day plans, which will abolish democracy and clamp down the rigid rule of the plutocrats over the workers, farmers, and all the common people.

In order to have a free hand for war and to rake in the huge profits promised by the war adventure, the plutocrats and their "Fifth Columns" are trying to weaken or abolish the Labor Relations Act, to destroy the right of organization and collective bargaining; they want to break down the Wages and Hours Law, and prevent its being extended to other workers. In this election, only the Communist Party shows the workers and progressive masses how these reactionary forces can be defeated, and labor's rights preserved and extended.

The enemies of the people and their "Fifth Columns" are fighting, openly and secretly, to prevent social legislation on behalf of the disinherited, the aged, the youth and the unemployed, and to weaken the present inadequate provisions for them. Only the Communist Party is willing to withhold from war purposes the necessary funds for old-age pensions of $60 per month after sixty years of age; for the American Youth Act, providing $5,000,000,000 for education and jobs to the young people; for expanded public works, employing at least three millions of the unemployed; for a real employment insurance system that will maintain the families of every worker unemployed through no fault of his own until he gets a job; for national health insurance, to guarantee a minimum of medical, dental, clinical, and hospital care for the entire population.

Our farming population is in perhaps the worst situation of all. Poverty is spreading in the countryside, and hundreds of thousands of farmers from old hardy pioneer stock are in peace-time America thrown into a position resembling that of the war refugees of Europe and China.

Only the Communist Party is willing to go to the necessary lengths to secure the land to the farmers, to lighten the tax burden on the family-size farms and to guarantee them cost of production for their crops, to provide cheap production credits, to remove the foreclosure threat of mortgages, to extend electrical and public service facilities to all the countryside, and to support co-operative marketing and production. This is because only the Communist Party is willing to place the burden where it belongs—on the great fortunes. But the people would be willing.

The rents now paid by the American people amount to enough to pay adequate returns on a capitalist basis, on a modern large-scale housing program that would house the whole American people. Only the Communist Party demands that idle capital and idle building workers be put on the job by the Government, to the tune of five billion dollars per year, to produce modern low-rent housing until every family has a decent home at low cost.

All these measures are absolutely necessary if the United States is to "produce a far higher standard of living for the masses." Yet the Democratic Party, which once put forth a much more modest housing project, has hastily withdrawn it in order to spend the money for a war in Europe, and neither the Republican nor any party except the Communist will adopt and fight for such a program as this one.

The Plutocrats Stand in the Way

One and all, the "great men" of our land, those who rule by virtue of owning the production plants of the nation, the economic royalists and all their political agents and "Fifth Columnists," unite in one answer to such a program: "The country could not afford it; it would lead the nation to bankruptcy."

But the same gentlemen who howl about "bankruptcy" when it is a question of investing a few billions of dollars in houses and healthy, strong, well-fed and well-clothed men, women and children, are exactly the same ones who blithely, without a moment's hesitation, vote more billions for airplanes, battleships, bombs and tanks, the only possible use for which is in a foreign war; they all agree upon war plans that envisage that the United States will spend twenty billions of dollars in war the first year. When it comes to war, their fears of "bankruptcy" disappear in dreams of war-time profits. Their motto is: "Billions for war, but not one cent to raise the American standard of living."

Why do you say that this country and this people cannot afford to go to work producing everything the country needs? Explain it to us more simply, you rich and wise and good gentlemen in whose stewardship America with all its untold riches has been placed? Why is it that America can afford twelve million idle workers; can afford forty million ill-housed, ill-clothed and ill-fed families; can afford mines, mills and factories closed down and rusting; can afford billions of capital lying idle in the banks; can afford accumulating agricultural surpluses, and to pay farmers to produce less; can afford to play the game of war, and can spend many billions preparing for war—but such a country cannot, you say, afford to put these men to work, to put these idle resources to work, because it would bankrupt us?

But you have admitted that such sums can be had; you wish to spend such sums for war.

Perhaps, if we can force you to try to explain this riddle, America will begin to see that there is nothing wrong with the productive resources of our country, nothing wrong with the workers and farmers, but that the whole trouble arises from the economic royalists, who stand as a barrier between the workers and the country's economy, and refuse to allow them to come together for the enrichment of the country, because you first must have your profit, a blackmail against production which is dragging the people deeper and deeper into unemployment, misery, poverty—and now into war!

No, the one thing America cannot afford is this war, this insane and catastrophic crushing of the lives of the millions who *are* America.

We are the best defenders of America, we the American workers and farmers, and the Communists in the very first ranks. We defend our country from its real enemies.

Nor can America afford the further development of the war hysteria which is rising to destroy the civil liberties and democratic rights of labor and the people. A great people's movement must assert itself in 1940, to demand with the Communists:

A People's Platform

Defeat every attempt to restrict freedom of speech, press, radio and assembly, and the right to organize and to conduct all activities of the trade unions to raise the standard of living of America.

Rouse the great masses to halt the attacks upon the trade unions, through anti-trust law indictments and "conspiracy" charges.

Demand the immediate enactment of the Federal Anti-Lynching Bill, which has been so shamefully pigeonholed by Congress and the Administration.

Secure the franchise to the Southern masses, white and Negro, by immediate Federal legislation prohibiting and penalizing all poll-tax laws and other limitations on the franchise, as a national issue, not a regional Southern issue, without the solution of which there is no effective democracy for the whole nation.

Abolish all discriminatory legislation and customs directed against the Negro population; unconditional equality, economic, political and social.

Defeat all the anti-alien legislation, and the so-called sedition laws, which are a modern resurrection in a worse form of the ancient "Alien and Sedition Laws" of the Administration of President Adams nearly one hundred and fifty years ago, in the fight against which Thomas Jefferson established American democracy, in the fight against which today this democracy can alone be preserved.

Defeat the attacks against the labor movement, which begin here as they did in Germany, with attacks on the Communist Party; these attacks constitute a knife at the throat of the Bill of Rights for the whole population.

Defend the Bill of Rights, which is even more important in time of war than in time of peace, which is a guarantee for all or is valid for none.

This immediate platform which the Communist Party offers to the country is not a revolutionary, not a socialist program.

Those who say that our country, with all its tremendous riches and productive forces, cannot realize such a plan should remember that such a program is being more than realized in a big country which only a few short years ago was ruined and poverty-stricken. It is true that it was not through capitalism, but instead through the new system of socialism, that the Soviet Union was able to multiply its national income tenfold during the past twelve years, and to raise the living standards of the masses by 500 per cent, while providing all necessary defense measures, with armed enemies all around on every border. But if capitalism is truly a system which makes it impossible to provide a better life for all the people, then that fact should be admitted, and the American people will have their opportunity to try out the new system of socialism which has proved that it can do so. Americans are as able and intelligent as any people in the world, and we can accomplish anything that has been accomplished elsewhere.

The crisis in America and the world has created a situation similar to that of 1856, when the dominant Whig and Democratic parties were, like the present dominant parties, divorced from the masses and in agreement to thwart their will—a situation which gave birth to a new party, a third party, which began as a desperate minority movement but swept to power in the nation four years later under Abraham Lincoln, solving the crisis through the abolition of slavery and the victory of the Union in the Civil War.

The masses of the United States cry out for such a new party, a modern Abraham Lincoln, as the only road toward the solution of the crisis of today, of the breakdown of capitalism, the crisis of imperialist war that threatens destruction to the world.

Accepting your nomination I pledge our Party to co-operate with labor and the people toward this goal.

Speech accepting the nomination for President at the Eleventh National Convention of the Communist Party of the United States, Madison Square Garden, June 2, 1940.

III. THE CONSCIENCE OF AMERICA

THE Veterans of the Lincoln Brigade have written an indelible page in the history of the American people. When the ruling class of America connived at the destruction of Spanish democracy, undermining the peace of the world, you, the sons of real America, the sons of the working class, came to the aid of the Spanish republic. When you placed your lives at the disposal of a cause which was the cause of all humanity, you gave something to America, something deep and powerful and lasting. Today, you who have come back to us have a particularly big and vital contribution to make to the peace and welfare of the American people. The biggest thing you have is the political lessons that the Veterans of the Spanish War have to give to the American people. You have a very special position in this country. I wonder if you realize what a very special position you occupy.

You are the men who with your own lives pointed the way, and, if it had been followed by our country, would have prevented the present world war. While you were in Spain, you were holding off this war from the world. The country could not see it; it refused to see it. Now it is paying the price. Europe is paying the price for the betrayal of the Spanish republic. Today most of America knows that the betrayal of the Spanish republic was not only a crime against Spain—that they always knew. Now they are beginning to realize that it was a crime against France, it was a crime against England, it was a crime against the United States, and that we are going to pay for this crime. We are going to pay long and bitterly.

If you want to realize what an important position you hold in relation to the development of the consciousness of the American people to this problem, just remember a few things that happened in the last months. You know, one of the big-shots in this country now is a fellow by the name of J. Edgar Hoover. He is a very powerful man, next to the President; his personage is sacred and his actions are shielded by the organized channels of public information and by the Government. Hoover can do almost anything he wants in America today. But Hoover found out that there is one thing he can't do—he can't put his hands on the Veterans of the Lincoln Brigade. When he tried it, he burned his fingers. That was because when he touched the Lincoln Brigade he touched the conscience of the American people and he had to pull his fingers back quick. What does that mean? It means that you can get the ear of the American people and can tell them things they won't listen to from anybody else.

The story told here about the meeting where the speakers were heckled and disturbed until the Veteran came forward to speak is a very significant little story. That is a symptom, a sign, a symbol of the position that all the Veterans hold in relation to all the American people. They listen to you when they won't listen to anybody else. But you can't speak clearly and systematically and effectively unless you are organized. That is why this organization becomes more and more important all the time. You must speak and you must make the American people hear what you have to say. It is vital for the American people, it is vital for the future of our country, it is vital for the future of the world.

There is another sign of how important it is that you should preserve and build your organization. If you want to know whether you have something valuable, one of the best tests is to see whether anybody else wants it. If nobody else wants it, you may become very careless of it. Well, you have been learning of late that there is somebody who wants the voice of the Veterans of the Spanish War. They want it for some very special purposes of their own. They want it so bad that although they did not give ten cents for the Veterans when they were soldiers in Spain, they are willing to give hundreds of thousands of dollars today to get a group of Veterans who will speak as they tell them to speak.

The Abraham Lincoln Brigade wrote a glorious page in history in Spain. Are the men who did that great job going to allow that little group who were the weak, who failed, who surrendered, and who betrayed, to be brought forward as the spokesmen of that great movement in the present world situation? I don't think you are going to allow it. And I think that the very threat of such a thing is going to be an additional reason for the Veterans to give a lot of new attention to the proper organization and functioning and work of this organization that you set up when you came back.

In addition to this great political task of transmitting your experiences and the results of your experiences to the American people, and first of all to the workers, to the labor movement, there is another big job which this organization can do best—save those men who are still in concentration camps in France. The treatment of the International Brigade members in France, together with the treatment of the Spanish refugees, is just one of the signs of the character of the French Government—a corrupt and reactionary gang of paid agents of the Two Hundred Families of French finance capital. But I think the time is approaching when more results can be gotten in rescuing our comrades from the clutches of this gang of gunmen and pirates which calls itself the French Government. I think it is possible to do something to get some action over there.

We have an especially outstanding clear example of the problem in the case of Gallo. Most of you know Gallo, I think—one of the finest workers ever produced; one of those natural military geniuses that the people can put forward every time they get a chance to display their initiative. If the French people had not their Weygands but a French Gallo in charge of the defense of France, there would be a different story in this war now. Gallo is sick and on the point of death. He is being kept in one of those filthy concentration camps and denied all help. Not only that—the Republic of Chile issued a visa for Gallo to come to Chile some time ago. The French Government refuses to let him go.

The government is always complaining that the refugees and veterans from Spain are a burden on the French people. Why don't they relieve some of that burden a little bit by letting Gallo go to Chile? Why do they insist on keeping him in a concentration camp? I think this one case of Gallo can prove the case for the whole four thousand International Brigade members in France and force a new policy on the French Government. The French Government is very sensitive to voices from America now. Those actions which many of you participated in at the French Consulate were listened to in Paris.

If they had been followed up more energetically, they might have gotten more results. Today the French Government is even more sensitive to voices from America. They can be made to hear them. They are more sensitive to these voices because their own position is more precarious than ever. Not precarious because of the military invasion—because when a government really represents the people, the harder oppressed the people are the more they unite around the government, the more solid that government becomes; but because the more the people begin to realize that the government is systematically selling them out that government becomes very unstable indeed. And the French people are already beginning to realize that the invasion of their country was not a simple military triumph.

The German break-through at Sedan was the fruits of treason in the French High Command. It was the Fifth Column at work. The French Government had been busy suppressing the trade unions and hounding the French Communists and throwing the Gallos into concentration camps, but the Fifth Column had a free hand in the highest ranks of the French army. And it was because the French people understood this that there was a shift in the cabinet and then a purge of the French High Command which involved fifteen generals. But if you think that this purging of the

French High Command means that now there is a new kind of defense of France, you had better think it over again. Because this purge was the sign of General Weygand's entrance into chief position of power in France.

General Weygand utilized the fact that the masses were aroused and angered and in revolt against the treason at the top in order to wipe out one set of military traitors to put in another set even worse than the ones he removed. Weygand is a Cagoulard. You know what the Cagoulards are? They are the French fascists, who were organized and financed by Hitler and armed by Hitler for civil war before this war began.

And yet there are people who want us in America to go over and help sustain that kind of a set-up. Well, some of them say that they only want us to send over our supplies, our airplanes, artillery, and so on. It is necessary to note, by the way, that if we had sent over a couple of thousand airplanes sixty days ago, Hitler would have had them today. Because through the help of the military command of the Allies in the last thirty days there were delivered into Hitler's hands more military supplies than the United States could produce in six months. And yet there are people who want to get the United States involved in that bloody mess over there. The ones who shout "Fifth Column" the loudest, and inflict concentration camps upon the International Brigade members and the workers and Communists, are themselves Hitler's Fifth Column, sitting in the offices of the Allied military forces. It is clear that the time is rapidly approaching in France when the French people are going to begin to take charge of their own defense.

And their first defense is going to be to clean out all these high gentlemen.

But we should not wait for that. When that takes place it will release Comrade Gallo and all of his fellows from the concentration camps. But let us not wait for that. Let us force Weygand·and Reynaud to release them even before the French people will. And the Veterans' organization can do more about this than anybody else because nobody dares to question their credentials. Who fought against Hitler and Mussolini when it was possible to defeat them and throw them back relatively cheaply—and once they had been thrown back the German and Italian people would have done the rest for us? It was the men who volunteered for the Spanish republic. Nobody can question your credentials. Nobody can dare to question them, and you have to take these credentials and go out and use them, and arouse the American workers and the American people to secure the release of the International Brigade Veterans from French concentration camps.

You have to use them to secure humane treatment for the Spanish refugees, while performing your detailed tasks here that arise out of your own immediate problems: to help organize that great majority of the American people that want to keep out of this imperialistic mess in Europe, to make their will effective, to make sure that the American people will not be thrown into any imperialist adventures abroad for any reason.

America will begin to overrule the gentlemen down in Washington who are dreaming of world conquest. America will begin to overrule those who are dreaming of great war profits. The American people will take advantage of this opportunity to join hands with all of those in Europe who are already fed up with the whole system and the whole class that produces this kind of war, and they will help to organize the world for peace instead of war.

The only kind of peace that can come out of this mess is the peace that removes not only the individual leaders that are responsible for these mass slaughters, but one that removes from power the whole class that is responsible for them.

Speech delivered at a meeting of Veterans of the Abraham Lincoln Brigade, June 7, 1940.

IV. THE MIDDLE CLASS AND THE WAR

AMERICA has the strongest class divisions in the world and it is least conscious of them. But whatever our lack of consciousness of the class nature of our society, the middle class and the working classes alike are going to realize that the world we have known in the past is disappearing before our eyes. It is destroying itself. The news from Europe is so shocking that even those of us who could foresee the awful consequences of the logical development of the imperialist world system find ourselves somewhat benumbed by the rapid succession of the blows of the old world tumbling about our ears.

In America we are now being invited to join that mad game in Europe. The invitations, which a few weeks ago were still coming only from the less experienced, already come from the chief executive of the nation. President Roosevelt's speech the night before last from Charlottesville practically was a declaration putting the United States into the world war. What it lacked in that respect was due to the formality needed by the constitutional provision that war must be declared by Congress.

The middle classes of America, together with the working class masses, have displayed a stubborn lack of enthusiasm for this war. I have been through two war periods myself. I was quite a youngster at the time of the Spanish-American war but I can remember it quite clearly. I was not quite so young during the last World War. And I can remember that much more clearly. In the previous wars, regardless of the manipulations behind the scenes that threw the country into the war, the ruling classes succeeded in rousing great mass enthusiasm for the war. There is no such enthusiasm in America for this war. And in order to slip this country, step by step, into the war, they have had to resort to the most foul deceptions. Each step leading America into the war was offered to the country as one of the means of staying out of the war. And even today they are trying to wring the last drop of profit out of this deception with the promise that America won't have to go to war.

War today is what they call a "total" war. There isn't such a thing as halfway in or halfway out. America's middle classes, as well as working class, may just as well make up their minds to that, if they don't want to be thrown head over heels into the war. If you don't want America to go through the dreadful experience that Europe is now enduring, you had better wake up and understand what is going on. Either this country is going to be all in or all out, and we would be better off if we stayed all out.

The war is being sold to the middle class on a promise that through entering the war we are going to preserve our way of life. The middle class is supposed to have found a comfortable way worthy of preservation. But the entrance of the United States into this war, no matter what the outcome in terms of the victory of one side or another, is inevitably going to wipe out forever that old "comfortable" middle class way of life. That is finished by this war and if America gets into it, it is finished for the American middle class too. If the middle class wants to preserve a while longer its way of life, it better wake up to the fact that there is only one way it can be done: Keep out of this war.

This war is the death struggle of the capitalist system. If America is so deeply involved in the death struggle of European imperialism that it cannot avoid jumping into the middle of it, participating in it, America will be taking the hard way, the most painful way to the future.

We need not be pessimistic about the future of the world at all. It is a painful thing to have to go through this period in which the dominant social and economic system is dissolving about us. It is a very destructive experience. But however destructive it may be, it cannot destroy the human race. It cannot destroy its intellectual achievements, it cannot destroy the tenacity, the determination and courage of the masses, and that greatest of achievements, the knowledge that a better world is possible and the knowledge of how to bring about that better world.

The war in Europe has definitely placed on the historical order of the day the socialist revolution. There is no other road whereby peace can be restored to Europe and the life of the peoples of Europe preserved. Peace can be brought to Europe only through the dethroning of the ruling classes of each and every belligerent country without exception. War-devastated Europe can be rebuilt only if the yoke of capitalist profit-making is removed from the neck of the European laboring people, and their creative ability is released; and the only way this is possible is through a socialist reorganization of Europe.

American capitalism is supposed to be stronger than that of Europe. It has achieved a higher development, so much so that America is practically equal in its productive forces to the rest of the capitalist world. American capitalist spokesmen and ideologists were of the opinion that the fate of this country is not necessarily and immediately tied up with the fate of the European systems. They used to tell us that the American way of life was superior and more stable than that of Europe. But these very same spokesmen are the ones today who come to us and tell us that the only way the American way of life can be preserved is by throwing America into the bloody imperialist mess in Europe. I would warn the gentlemen who give this message to America that they are accomplishing more in a few weeks than the Communist Party has been able to accomplish in twenty years in convincing the American people that we have got to think about a new social system for America. Because, if it is true that the only way to preserve the existing system in our country is through participation in this war, the American people, wanting no part in the war, are going to look for a system that will enable America to stay at peace.

Well, I should not object when the gentlemen of the bourgeoisie take over the tasks of the Communist Party in convincing the people that we have to have socialism in order to have peace. But I also know that these same gentlemen of the capitalist class, no matter how big a majority of the American people want peace, are going to carry us into war against the will of the people if they are permitted to do it.

Regardless of how big a majority of the American people would determine, as they will determine, that they want peace, even if it is necessary to establish socialism in America—if this is the only way we can have peace—these ruling class gentlemen will no more permit the people to make democratic decisions on socialism than they are now permitting a democratic decision on the question of war. They are going to give you no opportunity to vote on this question under the formal democracy of the American Constitution. They are first going to present you with an accomplished fact. And everyone who votes "no" is already being notified in advance that he is a traitor to his country. We are going to have a Hitler plebiscite on this question.

As a matter of fact, in the last few weeks we have traveled so fast on the road of fascism in the United States that it won't take us long to overtake and surpass Mussolini and Hitler. America always does things in a big way. And we are certainly doing things in a big way now. The destruction that has come to Europe will be brought to America, too, if we permit it. I say, if we permit it.

After all, Americans have not been in the habit—in their past history—of allowing entrenched ruling classes and cliques to put things over on them at a crucial moment.

Looking back at some of the most critical years of our history, it looked pretty hopeless for the future of our country as far back as 1850. It is very good to recall that history again. In the last four years of the 1850's we had a situation in which our country was at the crossroads: Were we going to develop as a slave nation or a free nation? And both major traditional parties of the country were agreed that America should in the main travel along the path of slavery. The masses of America were determined to take a different path, the path of free labor, the path of bourgeois democracy, and in that determination they represented that future of America which has been realized in the last eighty-five years and has made America economically the most powerful nation in the world.

But in the 1850's they faced, in all positions of power, entrenched reaction, those who were determined to make of America a slave country. Do you remember that the President of the United States in that period, Buchanan, was in league with the Secessionists of the South, using the office of President to prepare the destruction of the United States? Do you recall that the Congress in both houses was just as overwhelmingly in the control of the slave powers as the present Congress is controlled by those who are directing this country into the imperialist war? Do you remember that slave interests had complete control of the Supreme Court? And when after years of civil war, in order to carry through the measures to enable them to win the war, Lincoln had to pack the Supreme Court, enlarge it sufficiently to appoint a majority to overrule the adherents of the slave power and allow the American people to take the road of free development? The American people took that road. They smashed through overwhelming obstacles, they wiped out the slave power. They united America.

Lincoln is great in American history because he was the leader of the nation in that fight. He entered into that struggle as a proponent of compromise. He was determined to avoid the struggle, to compromise the struggle. It was the slave powers that forced him. Only after years of civil war and as a war measure did Lincoln issue the Emancipation Proclamation. But who can doubt today that, although Lincoln was not conscious in the first stages of the war of the tremendous cause that he was leading, the course of history and the will of the American people demanded the destruction and abolition of the slave system in America, even though this was carried through by a hesitating and reluctant instrument?

The American people can meet the present crisis with the same effectiveness as they met that crisis, the struggle against slavery. The present crisis is a deeper one. It is not only a national crisis, it is an international crisis. It is not only a crisis arising from one phase of the economic system, it is a crisis that goes to the very foundation of the social and economic system of the world except the Soviet Union, the only country that stands outside of this crisis.

In so far as the crisis is bound to grow more far reaching and more all-embracing, it requires determination and courage in order to meet and overcome it. Regardless of the complete lack of leadership from the traditional dominant parties, regardless of the fact that these parties are in the hands of the enemies of the people who are ready to sacrifice the people in this war, if only they can maintain their system of profits—regardless of these facts, allow me to express confidence that the American people are going to solve the crisis. And if they don't succeed in preventing the war-making capitalists from involving America in the war, they are certainly going to bring America out of the war, free from the rule of the war-makers, and it will be an America of the people at last.

Speech delivered at the meeting held under the auspices of the New Masses, June 12, 1940.

V. PERSECUTION BY LEGISLATION

On *July 10, 1940, Earl Browder, Communist candidate for President of the United States, appeared at his own request before a Senate Judiciary Subcommittee to state his opposition to the Voorhis Registration ("Blacklist") Bill.*

Present at the Senate Judiciary Subcommittee hearing when Earl Browder testified were Senators Tom Connally of Texas, Chairman, John E. Miller of Arkansas and John A. Danaher of Connecticut.—Ed.

Senator Connally: The Committee will come to order. This is another session of the subcommittee of the Judiciary Committee, holding hearings on H.R. 10094. I might say for the record that this hearing was called at the request of those persons who desired to appear, and the Committee has issued no compulsory process. The witnesses are here at their own invitation. I would like to know who is present this morning, wishing to appear.

Mr. Browder: Earl Browder, of the Communist Party.

Senator Connally: Mr. Earl Browder, of New York City; I believe that is right?

Mr. Browder: That is right.

Senator Connally: Is there anybody else who wants to appear? All right, Mr. Browder. Have a seat.

Senator Connally: Just give the reporter your name and official connections, if any.

Mr. Browder: Earl Browder, General Secretary of the Communist Party of the United States....

Senator Connally: Are you for the bill, or against it?

Mr. Browder: We are against this bill.

Senator Connally: All right, sir. Go ahead. . . .

Mr. Browder: On behalf of the Communist Party I would like to say about this bill, H.R. 10094, the so-called Voorhis Bill, that a study of this bill has given us the opinion that it represents, together with other measures of a similar sort before the Congress, a parallel to the Alien and Sedition Laws of the administration of President Adams at the close of the eighteenth century. This basic judgment is what determines our attitude on the bill as an attitude of opposition.

It differs of course from its ancient prototype in that the original Alien and Sedition Acts were quite boldly and openly directed against the rising democratic movement of the American people which culminated in the election of Thomas Jefferson, and was quite openly opposed to the development of democracy. The present bill with its companions puts itself forward as a support of democracy, and, in the name of defending democracy, proposes to limit and hamstring the democratic processes as they have developed in this country.

Senator Connally: Would it bother you if we interrupted you occasionally with questions, or would you rather go ahead and finish your statement and not have questions?

Mr. Browder: I think perhaps, while I have no objections to answering questions, it would be more fruitful for all of us if they came a little bit later.

Senator Connally: All right. We will be very glad to accommodate you, Mr. Browder. Go right ahead.

Mr. Browder: This Voorhis Bill is a typical example of the ambiguity of these modern attempts at the limitation of the democratic processes. Ostensibly directing itself against the agencies of foreign governments operating in American political life, this bill would actually result, if adopted and applied impartially, in outlawing a principle.

Senator Connally: A principle?

Mr. Browder: That is the principle of international working class organization, that principle of internationalism which Abraham Lincoln recognized and indorsed, when he said, responding to an address of the International Workingmen's Association, the First International, that (I quote from memory)—

The ties which bind the workingmen of all lands, of all races and of all nations are and should be the strongest, second only to the ties that bind people of one family and one kindred.

Let me make it clear to the Committee and for the record that the Communists are not opposed to the establishment of control over foreign agents within the United States. We recognize that in the present state of the world this is a problem that faces all countries. We do, however, see in the present bill before you, and in others of a related nature, that our country is being placed in danger of doing much more damage than could conceivably be done in the way of any service by these measures.

Specifically, we see in this act a concrete example of the attempts to take the United States along the same path of policy upon which France was taken immediately before, and after, especially, the outbreak of the present war. The sponsors of this bill have publicly cited the course of the French Government as an example which they wish to apply in their own way in America. It is therefore quite in order for us to give some attention to the significance of this course as it was applied in France, and the results of that course.

In France, there certainly were the so-called "fifth column" agents of foreign powers working within the political life of France, on a scale perhaps larger than ever seen in any other place. In fact, these so-called "fifth column" elements have seized power in France, and today constitute the effective government of that country. How did they come into power? It was not only that France was defeated in battle, because that defeat itself must be explained—and cannot be explained on military grounds. These foreign agents came to power in France first of all under the pretense that they were the leaders in the outlawing of treasonable organizations within France. They were the people who initiated the outlawing of the Communist Party of France. They were the people who suppressed, disrupted and disorganized the French labor movement. In fact, one can say the only efficient war measures taken by the French under the leadership of these so-called "fifth column" elements was the suppression of the labor movement and the Communist Party of France. Those measures, I submit to you, which are presented as a model for our country to follow, did not delay the coming to power of foreign agents within France over the French people. These measures initiated a whole course which hastened and was intended to hasten the military victory of the Nazis and the internal collapse of the French Republic.

From this concrete example, I would call your attention to the fact that Nazism and fascism of all varieties has risen to whatever degree of power it may have in any land always precisely under this flag—the suppression, outlawing of the Communist Party, first of all; second, the suppression or effective control over the labor movement, the organized trade unions; and, from that, proceeding to the destruction of all effective organizations of the masses of the people.

Senator Miller: Mr. Chairman, I want to ask the witness a question. I think I can do that without interrupting his chain of thought.

Senator Connally: All right.

Senator Miller: I just want to get the premise of your argument, there, Mr. Browder. As I understand it, you are basing or premising your objection to this bill upon the contention that the proponents of the bill may in fact be the subversive elements that will prevent the development of democratic processes in this country, is that right?

Mr. Browder: That would be a fair inference from the general line of my argument.

Senator Miller: That would follow?

Mr. Browder: Although I would not want to apply it mechanically.

Senator Miller: I know. I am applying it objectively, that is all.

Mr. Browder: In a general way.

Senator Miller: Yes. In other words, the statement that you made about France was as I understand it that the real subversive elements in France, or the "fifth column," that undermined France were operating behind the pretense that they were undertaking to suppress "fifth columnists"?

Mr. Browder: That is right.

Senator Miller: And therefore applying the same analogy to this?

Mr. Browder: Exactly, exactly.

Senator Miller: That is, that the men here undertaking to suppress "fifth columnists" or subversive activities in this country should be watched?

Mr. Browder: I think that is correct.

Senator Miller: I just wanted to get a clear understanding of your premise.

Mr. Browder: My reservation was this.... I think the political situation is so unclear and so confused in the United States that many honest people lend themselves to schemes, the ends of which they would by no means indorse, and which would appall them if they knew what they were doing.

Senator Miller: Yes. I understand your reservation.

Mr. Browder: I do not want to make any attacks, therefore, against any individuals.... Continuing with this general observation of the uniform course of the rise of Nazi and fascist forces in the world, I would point out that in every case the ideological character of these movements is to raise an intense and exclusive nationalism, the denial of any common international interests of the peoples of the world, and practically within the country to divert the political life of the country towards a struggle more and more intense against so-called "alien groups" within the country. In Germany it was first of all the Jews and the Marxians—the so-called "Marxians"—and all those who recognize common international interests among peoples.

We have had long experience in American history with such

issues. This is not new to our country. I have already mentioned that in the 1790's Thomas Jefferson was denounced as an agent of the French Revolution, and the Alien and Sedition Laws of that time were based upon the theory that the rising democratic movement in the United States was merely an extension of and an agency of the French Revolution, and specifically of the Jacobin Clubs of France, which were paralleled in the United States by the democratic clubs that founded the original party of Jefferson called the "Republican Party," and later, the "Republican-Democratic Party" of that time. In fact, the Society of Tammany was one of the organizations which were outlawed by the Alien and Sedition Acts of that time.

We have further the experience of one of the most dangerous periods in the life of our country, in the decade just before the Civil War. The whole political life of our country was distorted by the movement that was generally identified under the name of the "Know Nothing" movement, which almost created an atmosphere of civil war in the United States on very false issues, central among which was the campaign against the Catholics as agents of a foreign power in American political life. This theme has repeated itself again and again since that time. The Ku Klux Klan type of influence in American life lives upon this sort of thing, and while it is an old influence in America it is by no means comprised within that body of doctrine or ideology which is generally accepted as Americanism. It is the enemy of the best traditions of our country. This, we consider it should be pointed out, is the most dangerous influence in our country, the most to be guarded against; and this influence is not combated but rather expresses itself in the bill under consideration, and others of like nature. This trend represents not the combating of dangerous influences but the writing of their essential position into the law of the land—not the combating of Nazi influences, but the registration of a victory of Nazi influence in the political life of our country.

I know of course that it will be pointed out that this bill in its application not only strikes at legitimate political parties in the

United States like the Communist Party, but that it would also create organizational difficulties for the German-American Bund, for example.... Any incidental embarrassment that this bill might give to the Bund would be much more than offset by the political victory it would represent for the Nazi philosophy under which the Bund operates.

Senator Connally: Well,... are you assuming to speak for the Bund as well as for the Communist Party?

Mr. Browder: I am speaking as an observer of politics in America, who presumes to pass judgment on the influence of this bill upon the whole political life of our country. I speak against the Bund and against this bill as representing an identical political tendency....

The next point I will direct myself towards on this bill is its ambiguity. Hypocrisy and ambiguity are the most dangerous things in the making of laws. Objects to be achieved by laws should be clearly defined. This is not the case with the bill under consideration. If this law should be enacted we would be faced with the alternative, either, first, the law would not be impartially applied ... or, if it were impartially applied, it would create such results that I am sure the sponsors of this bill would not accept them as the legitimate consequences of their acts, because, impartially applied, this bill would make it impossible for the trade union movement as at present constituted in America to operate.

Senator Connally: There have not been any labor representatives here protesting against it. They do not object to it.

Mr. Browder: I think they assume that this bill will not be impartially applied; and perhaps the assumption is not so far-fetched. By the terms of the bill, however, it includes the whole labor movement of America, and places them under such obligations that the trade union movement of America as at present constituted could by no means, no matter how much they wanted to, comply with this law. It is an impossibility to come under the terms of this law and comply with its provisions.

Senator Connally: Well, would you mind talking more about

your own Party and its objections, and why it would put you out of business, rather than the trade unions. We will look after those, later.

Mr. Browder: I think I should first speak about the trade unions, because the danger with regard to the trade unions is much greater than that with regard to the Communist Party. After all, our Party is a small, weak organization, relatively uninfluential in the affairs of our country, and if our words have any importance, it is not because we talk about ourselves or our own particular position.... While not at all speaking on behalf of the trade unions, it is necessary for any responsible person in public life to point out that the measures before us, if impartially applied....

Senator Connally: That connotes an assumption in your mind that it is not going to be impartially enforced.

Mr. Browder: I was pointing out alternatives. The first alternative is that the bill may not be impartially applied, in which case of course the bad results of it would be narrowed, because the bad results would come only where it was applied.... The other alternative is to assume that it would be impartially applied.... In that case it would render impossible the operations of the trade union movement as at present constituted....

It may suffice to point out that any form of international affiliation brings an organization under the terms of this act and responsible for the fulfilling of some fourteen points of obligations to Governmental instances,...I challenge any organization in America to state through its responsible officers that it could possibly fulfill those fourteen points under any circumstances.

Thus, we have the ambiguous character of this bill brought before us in its most obvious form, that it attempts by indirection to accomplish what evidently is understood cannot be properly defended directly before the Congress or the country. It creates obligations on organizations which have any form of organizational recognition of the principles of the international common interests of the working people of the world, and upon such organizations it places obligations which are impossible of fulfillment by any organization in America. There is no functioning political organization in America that could possibly meet the requirements of the fourteen points listed in this law, beginning on page 5 and ending on page 7. It is not possible to operate under that law without constantly violating the law and subjecting every leader and every member of that organization to a fine of $10,000 or imprisonment for five years....

Senator Miller: Mr. Browder, in reference to your objection to the fourteen points, now, I can visualize some trouble in complying with or furnishing the information required by the fourteen points, by certain organizations, but now let us see if there would be any actual trouble in furnishing the information required in the fourteen points, beginning on page 5, down to the middle of page 7, with the organizations that would be required to file the information, going back to page 3, that it is only directed first to every organization subject to foreign control.

Mr. Browder: The foreign control, if you will pardon my interrupting—

Senator Miller: Yes.

Mr. Browder: —is defined.... It is defined to include this. "Foreign control" means any organization which in any way has any affiliations outside of the United States.... "Any affiliations outside of the United States" is defined as "foreign control...." That means that under Section 1 is included not only the Communist Party but the American Federation of Labor....

Senator Connally: Well, it is not complaining of it.

Mr. Browder: No, it is not complaining, because it does not expect the law to be applied; but those are the terms of the law....

I would have to raise very serious questions as to how such laws would be applied, because we have had the experience, if you will pardon me, Senator, of seeing excellent laws, taking them as they appeared on paper, in France, and in Germany in the early years before the Nazis came into power, laws ostensibly directed towards the rising of these anti-democratic movements, which in application were applied only to the Communist Parties of those countries; so while I would have to admit the correctness in principle of the position you have stated, I would have to put my reservations very seriously as to how those principles would be applied....

Senator Connally: Would not France have been a lot better off if she had known in advance the international relationships that were going on between the "fifth column" in France and the influences in other countries, before the debacle of the French Republic?

Mr. Browder: France knew it.

Senator Connally: Well, if she knew it, she did not make any use of it.

Mr. Browder: That is the trouble.... The Communists were the only people in France that voted against the Munich betrayal....

Finally, let me make it clear that if the Communist Party comes under the terms of this bill it is not because the Communist Party in any way is under foreign control.... I can remark in passing that in my opinion it is clearly unconstitutional, and I would expect that four or five years of its enforcement would finally bring a Supreme Court decision that it was unconstitutional and illegal; but that would not be of very much help for the immediate situation before the country....

One last word. I do not think that the argument that I have presented is an argument directed towards protecting the Communist Party against attacks which it would experience under such a law as this, except in the most incidental way. I direct all of my arguments primarily to the preservation of the political life of our country. The harm that would be done to the Communist Party would be purely incidental but the harm that would be done to the whole political life of America by such measures as this would not be remediable under the present world situation for a very long time. It would distort the whole political development of our country in facing the world crisis. It would stultify the thinking of our country. It would place under the ban of illegality some of the most important issues and programs which America must debate in the coming period and in advance of such debates try to determine its outcome by prejudging it, placing certain views under the ban.

We have confidence in American democracy that it can consider all of these issues and arrive at a correct decision. We do not think that you have to control the thinking processes of the American people in order to guarantee the outcome. . . .

Abridged stenographic report of the Senate Judiciary Subcommittee, Senate Office Building, Washington, D. C., July 10, 1940.

VI. THE PAN-AMERICAN CONFERENCE

ON JULY 20 there meets in Havana a conference of the twenty-one American republics, called on the initiative of the Roosevelt Administration. The declared purpose of the conference is to achieve a common approach of the Americas to the problems raised by the imperialist war.

Certainly there are common interests of the peoples of the twenty-one American republics; and equally certain it is that these common interests are placed in special jeopardy by the chaotic world conditions. It is therefore a very immediate and real set of problems which furnish the setting for the Havana conference, problems which will increasingly affect directly the lives of close to a quarter billion population, and indirectly the course of world history.

Secretary of State Cordell Hull is reported by the newspapers to have issued an angry warning to Nazi Germany to keep its hands off the Havana conference. It is freely declared in the capitalist newspapers that Nazi influences threaten to create difficulties in the conference.

How is it possible that German influence can become the central issue within a conference of the twenty-one American republics?

There are two chief factors which make this possible. They are, first, conflicting interests between the Government of the United States, on the one hand, which reflects the interests of United States finance capital, and the Latin American countries, on the other hand, whose governments reflect interests within their own countries in conflict with the aims and policies of Washington. Second, there is a broad range of differences and conflicts within

Latin America itself, which are more or less clearly reflected in the policies of their governments which will be represented in Havana. It is because of the existence of these contradictions and conflicts among the twenty-one American republics that German and other non-American influences are a major problem in Havana.

Let us examine these two main sources of conflict in Havana in more detail, taking up first that between the United States and the Latin American countries as a whole.

A glance at the historical background of United States-Latin American relations will throw much light upon our own immediate problems. These relations have developed for over a hundred years under the Monroe Doctrine, which is supposed to indicate a long-time uniform policy. But surface uniformity only hides the most deep-going historical transformations that have changed the contents of the policy into the opposite of what it was originally.

During the nineteenth century, the chief significance of the Monroe Doctrine lay in its character as a support to the national liberation movement of the Latin American peoples, in their struggles to break away from the old European semi-feudal empires. It was an instrument of the bourgeois-democratic revolution. But the most complete and successful bourgeois-democratic system, the U. S. A., rapidly came under the dominance of finance-capital, of monopoly. The turning point marking the emergence of the United States as a modern imperialist power was characterized by the twin events: the Spanish-American War and the formation of the U. S. Steel Corporation.

From that time on, the Monroe Doctrine was merely the historical costume used to dress up the new policy of imperial conquest of Wall Street, of finance capital, of monopoly, constantly extending its power over the earth, but first of all and most ruthlessly into Latin America. The high-handed, illegal seizure of Panama was an outstanding example, covering up the most reactionary political and social consequences with the glories of the great technical achievement of the Panama Canal. The cruel fate of Puerto Rico as a United States possession after its seizure from Spain disclosed modern imperialism as even more ruthless than the old semi-feudal empires, because of its more far-reaching economic consequences.

The shelling of Vera Cruz by Woodrow Wilson's order in 1916, and the invasion of Mexico by John J. Pershing's army, left a deep wound in the relations between the United States and all Latin America, as did the occupation of Haiti, the war against Sandino in Nicaragua, the imposition of the Platt Amendment upon Cuba —to mention only a few of the most well-known and dramatic phases of United States conquest over Latin America, which expressed and carried forward the more pervasive penetration of U. S. capital and the conquest of Latin American economic life.

It was not out of imagination, but from prolonged bitter experience, that the Latin American people raised their slogans against "Yankee Imperialism" and the "Colossus of the North."

If today the agents and spokesmen of Nazi Germany can conjure up these powerful spirits against Pan-American unity at Havana, for their own ends, let us clearly understand that the United States is paying the inevitable price for the crimes of its own imperialist masters. It is no remedy to do as Secretary Hull and the U. S. press are doing—to curse the Germans and denounce as Nazi helpers all those who mention these historical sore spots in U. S.-Latin American relations. So long as these problems are denied or ignored they will become only worse, not better. If Havana is to mark a step in the direction of a real Pan-American unity in the interests of the peoples, that can be achieved only if decisive steps are taken away from the old policies of exploitation by the United States.

If the United States were ready to demonstrate by its policies and deeds that it is really opening a new chapter of helpful interrelations among the American peoples, then it would have nothing to fear from the manipulation of old grievances by any non-American power. But the very fear and hysteria displayed in Washington at the prospect of such non-American influences is itself a sign that Washington has no intention of further developing a "good neighbor" policy, but on the contrary intends more decisively than ever to drive ahead on the old imperialist lines. Washington's fears are primarily fears of the results of its own policies.

When we turn to examination of the concrete proposals which have been given to the press by Washington, in anticipation of the Havana conference, we are confirmed in our presumption that the Roosevelt Administration has plumped hook, line and sinker for an intensified imperialist policy.

The chief proposal publicly mentioned has been the formation of a huge Pan-American Bank together with a marketing monopoly to handle all Latin American export surpluses.

Clearly, these interrelated projects are extremely desirable from the point of view of U. S. ruling circles, the banks and industrial monopolies. By the mere weight of their financial and economic resources, they would thereby grasp at once such power over all the Americas as they now exercise over the U. S. But by the same token, the Latin American peoples will approach these proposals with the utmost reserve. Latin America needs the help of the United States, even as we need the co-operation of Latin America, but the peoples of all the Americas will suffer deeply from such crude and obvious projects of monopoly exploitation as the proposed Bank and Marketing Cartel under the Wall Street domination.

Even if it should be assumed that the projects are practically feasible, in their broadest economic aspect, which is more than doubtful in view of the collapse of all U. S. schemes for handling its own surplus products, they would inevitably subordinate Latin American national economies to that of the United States.

Is that line of development in the interests of the Latin American nations and peoples? Clearly it is not, but rather the opposite. The only salvation of the Latin American nations lies in the direction of a progressively increasing economic independence, to be achieved through (1) their own industrialization and reclaiming their economies from foreign ownership; (2) a more balanced agriculture; (3) the development of foreign trade between the Latin American countries; and, (4) prevention at all costs that any one of the great capitalist powers should secure monopoly over their foreign trade with the rest of the world.

These are the indispensable conditions which the Latin American people must secure in any large-scale and long-time agreements with the United States. These conditions have been given no consideration as yet in the proposals from Washington. That is the primary difficulty facing the Havana conference.

It is worthy of special note that on this issue, the interests of the people of the United States, as distinct from those of the financiers and monopolists, coincide with the interests of the Latin American peoples. We in the United States cannot successfully break the chains of monopoly over our own life if we help to bind Latin America in similar but even heavier chains. Wall Street's super-profits from Latin America only help to grind down the people of the United States into deeper poverty and oppression.

It must be further noted that the present foreign trade of Latin America is necessarily directed in the first place, not to the United States, but to Europe and Asia. The United States is a competitor with, not a market for, the main body of Latin American exports. If the United States proposes to take over the marketing of those exports, it is not at all to find a market within the United States, but rather in order to control the relations of Latin America with the rest of the world, to assume a guardianship or protectorate over Latin America. But Latin American interests, so long as we are operating under the capitalist system, cannot be merged thus with those of the United States Colossus, without irremediable harm to all the peoples involved. Faced with a series of great capitalist imperialist powers, British, German, Italian, Japanese and United States, the Latin American nations must first of all strive unitedly for their freedom from domination by any one of them, preserving their economic and political freedom of action to utilize the contradictions between them to defeat them all in their efforts at domination. Latin America cannot afford to trade this freedom for paper guarantees by the United States, which have a validity equal to, but no more than, the British guarantees to Czechoslovakia, Austria, Norway, Belgium, Holland, France and China.

The Latin American peoples should make their voices heard at

Havana, placing these demands and considerations before the world, and specifically before the United States. If the U. S. Government can be brought to a policy which places Latin America firmly on the road to its own independence and progress, in contrast to that now operative, then and then only will we be moving toward that Pan-American unity which all the peoples need and strive for; then and then only can ever closer economic relations with the United States serve the cause of all the peoples.

Most sinister and dangerous of all the hidden motives at work behind the scenes at Havana is the determination of American imperialists to harness Latin America to their war plans, to their preparations to plunge the Americas into the armed struggle for the redivision of the world.

The imperialist war creates a real threat to Latin America. But the most immediate danger arising from the war is the danger that the Americas will be dragged into the slaughter by the Wall Street forces represented by the Roosevelt Administration and equally by the Republican nominee for the Presidency, Wendell Willkie. The Havana conference is intended as a step in this direction. The peoples must look to the Latin Americans to defeat the war-making objectives in the conference. This danger has not disappeared with Roosevelt's "pledge" not to send American soldiers to Europe, which came only after the last possibility of doing so had disappeared. There is more than one way of plunging the Americas into the world war, and Washington will try all of them.

The recent furore and shouting about the Monroe Doctrine was directed mainly to the attention of Germany. But history has perpetrated one of her little ironies, by presenting the first concrete case in the form of the British violation of French sovereignty in the West Indies, in the attempt to head off American planes from reaching France and being used against Britain. This is of one piece with that great joke history has played, in which Roosevelt's great campaign to arm the Allies has resulted in Hitler's possession of more American fighting planes than the U. S. army itself possesses.

At Havana the Latin Americans should establish more firmly the principle that the Monroe Doctrine has no longer any validity except as the expression of voluntary agreements of the American republics; these should establish the means of self-determination for the peoples of territories now held as colonies. Only thus can the Americas be closed against the European war.

Finally, it is necessary to note that the Latin American Governments are themselves of such widely variegated political character as to promise much confusion and a minimum of agreement at Havana. Formally all twenty-one governments represented are republics; but few represent popular and democratic regimes. Many are crude minority dictatorships, representing small privileged classes of bourgeoisie and landlords. Brazil and Argentina, with some smaller republics, are dominated by British capital, with strong German influences, and in the event of a British-German settlement, will in all probability plump wholeheartedly for a place in the European fascist alignment.

This is the real nightmare of the U. S. imperialist circles, which really fear German penetration of Latin America only when it is combined with the British. The only really popular and democratic regimes in Latin America, even in a limited sense, are those of Cuba, Chile and Mexico, although there are promising democratic movements in several other countries. It would therefore be utopian to expect the Havana conference to give more than a distorted expression to the interests and needs of Latin America, while the people of the United States will be completely misrepresented, probably in the person of our American Ribbentrop, Sumner Welles.

The Havana conference can and must be the occasion, however, for a great campaign of education of the peoples on the conditions for and problems of a real people's Pan-American unity.

Out of such a people's movement alone will come the salvation of the Americas from imperialist domination and war, and the building of the Americas as a stronghold of progress, prosperity and peace.

Daily Worker, *July 19, 1940.*

PART TWO

THE MOST PECULIAR ELECTION

I. THE COURT STEPS IN

As a candidate for President of the United States, I have been denied by court order the right to accept invitations to speak to citizens who wish to forward my candidacy. This court order was made on the request of the Administration, undoubtedly with the agreement, if not upon the direct suggestion, of the President. Judge Knox, in issuing the order, said openly that his motive was political—to hamper the Communist Party in placing its position before the voters. He charged that the Communist Party was not entitled to any consideration because "it proposes to change the form of government of the United States."

Judge Knox did not take notice of the fact that it is President Roosevelt who has successfully set aside the Constitution of the United States, and effectively changed our form of government, by committing this country to a war alliance and to belligerent steps without even the formality of submitting the question to Congress. If Congress can be set aside so completely by the new military dictatorship now apparently in power on issues involving the fate of the nation most immediately, we must not be surprised when individuals and minority parties are deprived of all rights by administrative edict. When a "close friend of the President" threatened last October to stop my speaking in public on behalf of the Communist Party, most people thought we were exaggerating when we marked that moment as opening a drive into war and military rule for America. Now the facts are clear for everyone. Not only are the Communists disfranchised, but even the Republicans, who are forced to choose between two Democrats; and not only the Republicans, but the anti-war, anti-conscriptionist majority of Americans, who are forced to choose between two pro-war and pro-conscriptionist candidates. Mr. Roosevelt has studied well the Hitlerian art and bids fair to outdo the record of his teacher.

My own little problems are of interest to the American people because they embody in essence the great tragedy of a whole nation —tricked into the chains of a gang of military adventurers as surely and as disastrously as were the German people.

Statement issued September 4, 1940, on Federal Judge Knox's order denying Earl Browder the right to leave the jurisdiction of the Court.

II. THE MOST PECULIAR ELECTION CAMPAIGN IN THE HISTORY OF THE REPUBLIC

Our country is supposed to be going through that supreme process of American democracy, the election of a President. But this is the most peculiar election campaign in the history of our republic. An illuminating aspect of this peculiar character is the nature of this, my speech, and its manner of delivery to you. I am forced to speak to you through a phonograph disc, because a Federal judge, Mr. Knox by name, granted the demand made by the representative of another candidate, Mr. Roosevelt by name, that I should be forbidden to travel over the country to make speeches for my own candidacy and party and against Mr. Roosevelt's candidacy and party. I was threatened with immediate imprisonment if I should dare to come to the Pacific Coast to speak to you in this election campaign. Therefore I am forced to speak in this unusual fashion, which is unsatisfactory, but at least serves to point a moral.

Judge Knox, in granting Roosevelt an order to silence a rival candidate, used as an excuse that I have been convicted of a crime, in a case which is now before the Supreme Court. But neither he nor the newspapers will tell you, although it is a fact they well know, that the Roosevelt Administration was more than willing to forget that supposed crime, as the Hoover Administration had done in 1930, if I and my party would only continue to support Roosevelt in 1940 as we had done in 1936, 1937 and 1938. They used the charge against me as political blackmail. They thought they could whip the Communist Party into line, in spite of their

85

war policies, in spite of conscription, in spite of their Sherman Act prosecutions of the trade unions, in spite of the scuttling of the New Deal, in spite of their renewed alliance with the "economic royalists." They thought they could handle the Communist Party as they handle Tammany in New York, or the Kelly machine in Chicago, or the Hague machine in New Jersey.

But they made two mistakes: first, they had no charges against the Communist Party or myself involving moral turpitude, or any damage to individuals or government, as they have been forced to admit officially, nothing in fact like the reeking record of the men who renominated Roosevelt in Chicago at the Democratic Convention, and nothing of which we are ashamed; and, secondly, the Communist Party cannot under any circumstances be blackmailed or coerced into the slightest support, direct or indirect, of policies or candidates against the interests of the working people who make up a great majority of America. Now, realizing its mistakes, the Roosevelt Administration is as viciously hostile to the Communist Party as formerly it was friendly and helpful to us when it needed and received our help. *But we are the same Party; it is not we who have changed, but rather the Roosevelt Administration.*

"America's First Dictator"

Roosevelt's agent, Knox, said the Government could not allow me to travel over the country because I had been convicted of a crime in traveling under my own name after I had, years ago, traveled under assumed names in Europe and Asia as a protective measure, for reasons of safety. But the same courts, and the same Roosevelt Administration, freely grant permission to travel anywhere to real criminals under appeal, such as Judge Manton who for years sold to the highest bidder the decisions of the Federal Courts of New York, and elsewhere, such as Moe Annenberg, the multi-millionaire racketeer Republican whose financial connections with the Democratic machines of New Jersey and Chicago are matters of public gossip. In fact, it is a settled policy of the Government to permit free movement of persons under bail pending appeal; but in my case, the Roosevelt Administration openly excuses its unprecedented action by a political argument, saying it is because I and my party "propose to change the form of government of the United States," and for this reason do not deserve the consideration given to common criminals.

But who is really changing the form of government of the United States? It is the Roosevelt Administration, under the direct leadership of the President himself. They have been deliberately violating the election laws and the Constitution itself, throwing the Communist Party and other minor parties off the ballot in state after state, in order to steal Communist votes they may need to win the elections, and in order more effectively to silence our voices. And it was the President himself who, on September 3, openly stepped outside the Constitution, assumed the powers of an unlimited military dicator, committed the United States to a military alliance with Great Britain and participation in the second imperialist war—all without even the formality of submitting the issues to Congress, which under the Constitution alone holds the power of making alliances and deciding questions of war and peace. Even such a sober and conservative newspaper as the St. Louis *Post-Dispatch* opened its editorial judgment on these steps with these words: "Mr. Roosevelt today committed an act of war. He also became America's first dictator."

And concludes that:

And all this is done in utmost contempt of democratic processes and of the Constitution of the United States.

If this secretly negotiated deal goes through, the fat is in the fire and we all may as well get ready for a full-dress participation in the European war.

If Roosevelt gets away with this, we may as well say good-bye to our liberties and make up our minds that henceforth we live under a dictatorship.

If Congress and the people do not rise in solemn wrath to stop Roosevelt now—at this moment—then the country deserves the stupendous tragedy that looms right around the corner.

This is the Roosevelt whose agents cry about the Communist Party, that it must be denied electoral rights, and even outlawed, because forsooth "it proposes to change the form of government of the United States!"

With a Congress which permits, and even invites, such a peremptory shearing of its constitutional powers, which cannot even protest when on the question of war it is placed in the position of a Hitler Reichstag, we must not be surprised that the new Roosevelt dictatorship proceeds roughly and crudely to deprive individuals and minority parties of all political rights. The suppression of the Communist Party is a necessary and important part of the gigantic conspiracy to effectively disfranchise the majority of the American people. Last October, when Roosevelt, speaking to the newspapers through a "close friend," threatened me with legal action to stop my public speaking, most people thought we exaggerated when we said that threat opened a drive into war and military dictatorship for America. Now the facts are clear for everyone. Every nation that has lost its liberties started on the downward path with the act of suppressing the Communists. Roosevelt is following the Hitler formula with scientific exactitude.

The Roosevelt-Willkie Conspiracy

It is not only the Communists who are being disfranchised in 1940. The New Deal masses and the labor movement are left politically homeless. The Republicans are worse off than we, for they have not even a candidate to fight for; they must either vote for a Democrat, or turn to the Communists. The leading and natural candidate of the Republican Party was Robert A. Taft. But he was defeated in the Philadelphia Convention, and the pro-war, Big Business, renegade Democrat, Wendell Willkie, was nominated by a conspiratorial junta, organized by Thomas W. Lamont of the firm of J. P. Morgan, working in direct agreement with Roosevelt, and engineered by Walter Lippmann. Willkie was chosen for the Republican Party by Roosevelt and Lamont after an agreement had been reached as to fundamental policy to which all would adhere, the same policy revealed in the President's sensational coup of September 3.

Willkie's nomination was the guarantee which Roosevelt required before he dared to launch his coup d'etat. The masses, the majority of the voters, had to be disarmed, denied every opportunity of effective protest, before the President dared to proclaim the joining of the United States into the British Empire. Even now, with the elections effectively blocked off from the people, Roosevelt dares not submit his secretly matured plans to a vote of Congress, but must act by proclamation, by edict, by a coup d'etat.

In its cunning trickery, in its cynical betrayals, in the personal character of its leading participants, the Roosevelt coup d'etat is in the historical tradition of Louis Napoleon; in its social significance for today, it is a flagrant adaptation of the technique of Adolf Hitler; in its consequences for the American people it is a catastrophe expressing the most profound and violent crisis of the capitalist world.

Imagine, for one moment, what would be the reactions of the great body of American voters to the Roosevelt coup if the Republican Party had nominated as its candidate Senator Robert A. Taft, that old-fashioned conservative Republican who voted against the conscription law! Can anyone doubt that the result would have been such a Republican landslide as would have wrecked the Democratic Party for all time? In that comparison, you get the full significance of the Willkie candidacy, which can be understood only as preparation for the Roosevelt coup. Even with this set-up, Willkie is hard pressed with the danger that the masses may transform his formal opposition to Roosevelt into a channel for expression of their deep abhorrence of the war and conscription, their deep disgust with Roosevelt's machinations, and to prevent this he is reducing his campaign to a hollow mockery, which only with difficulty can win a headline in the newspapers pledged to his election.

This is the political set-up for the 1940 Presidential elections, which brings the decisive leaders and controlling forces of both Democratic and Republican parties to look upon the Communist Party, despite its small numbers and meager resources, as a major danger to their joint aims; this is what unites them in the vicious efforts to drive the Communist Party off the ballot and to suppress its activities, to silence its voice. With both major parties united in thwarting the will of the vast majority of the people, they sense the danger and the possibility that millions of voters could, given the opportunity, cast votes of protest for the only party that clearly denounces their conspiracy of war and reaction, and which gives practical alternative policies—the Communist Party.

The "Fifth Column" Camouflage

To cover up their real fears of the workers, of the majority of the people, the Democratic-Republican coalition justifies its persecution of the Communist Party by a wild newspaper campaign branding us as part of a "Fifth Column" of the enemies of the country. That also has the aim to hide the operations of the real Fifth Column, which in every country has been proved to have its head and motive force in the upper classes, and among the workers has only degenerated Socialist leaders, Trotskyites, and such-like riffraff. Such real Fifth Column elements are flooding into the United States now; they seem to have little difficulty in obtaining visas or in operating freely when here. We even see U. S. naval vessels bringing their choicest specimens to our shores. We are entitled to begin asking some questions about this real Fifth Column in America, and to inquire what sort of new surprises they are hatching up for the American people in collaboration with our native reactionaries.

For example, rumor has it that the United States is now host to a certain distinguished Frenchman, a big industrialist and close personal friend of Marshal Petain, head of the French government of capitulation to Hitler. This visitor to our shores is head of a great French trust which up until June of this year was furnishing Germany with essential materials for her airplane production, the supply never ceasing, for in June the Germans came in and took direct possession. This distinguished Frenchman was considered important enough to receive the personal attention of a select group of big bankers, and a special visit from Mr. Stettinius, after which, rumor has it, he is on a tour of inspection of American armaments and armament industries. Many newspaper men are wondering why they received strict instructions not to report or comment upon this gentleman's arrival in this country, or his activities since his arrival. He is evidently a person of mysteriously great importance. His presence here doubtless indicates some possible new surprises in the unpredictable international situation, which may not be altogether agreeable to the American people. The President has called upon the public to report the activities of suspicious persons, possible Fifth Columnists; may we presume to suggest that the mystery that surrounds this peculiar visitor should be dispelled for the general public? Not to mention, in this connection, the horde of British agents, of whom only Sir George Paish received dishonorable mention in the Senate.

WALL STREET'S REAL AIM

The mystery that surrounds these high-placed Fifth Columnist visitors is equaled by the mystery of aims that guide the White House. Where is our country being headed? Roosevelt has been less than frank with the country, ever since he proclaimed neutrality last September and then systematically proceeded to break down that neutrality. But not all high sources are so evasive about the future perspective. Allow me to quote some little known declaration from those "in the know."

The *Army and Navy Journal* of August 24 declares:

The inevitable conclusion to be drawn from these developments is that the United States has moved to the point where it is committed to assist the British Empire in the war against Germany. . . . Only the blind can fail to see that the United States is rapidly moving toward participation in the world struggle ... [for] an Empire greater than any which history has ever known.

That is the bald and unadorned truth underlying the sickening propaganda about the defense of democracy and civilization. Wall Street is on the march toward "an empire greater than any which history has ever known." Roosevelt is leading the march, and scattering the wreck of even the limited democracy of the American Constitution along the way. Willkie is his first assistant in the conspiracy against the well-being and very lives of the common people. Of all organized political bodies in the United States, only the Communist Party exposes and combats this gigantic imperialist counter-revolution. That is why Roosevelt and Willkie, and all their helpers, are determined to crush the Communist Party first of all. That is why Oscar Wheeler, a West Virginia farmer, was sent to prison for fifteen years for the crime of soliciting signatures to put the Communist Party on the ballot.

That is why the Communist candidate for President was sentenced to prison on an ancient and trumped-up technical charge, and is now refused the right to travel to address your meeting, although the case is before the Supreme Court. That is why the hysteria against the foreign-born workers, and against the labor movement which opposes conscription, is being whipped up to a typical fascist fury. But that is also why the great majority of the American people, regardless of their opinions about a future socialism or communism for America, must rally to the defense of the Communist Party as the only way they can fight for their own rights and aspirations in 1940. Only the Communist Party provides the opportunity in the 1940 elections to register the sentiments of the people against the imperialist conspiracies, against the war policies, against the black reaction that has risen to power in the Roosevelt dictatorship.

The economic royalists and their servants are riding high, and gleefully congratulate themselves that the masses have been hogtied, that nothing can now spoil their plans for a great imperialist speculation with the blood and lives of the American people. But the fight is only begun. Notwithstanding all difficulties and hardships, the American people cannot forever be tricked, bulldozed and suppressed. They are fighting back with increasing numbers, energy, intelligence and determination. And the final victory will belong to the people.

Speech delivered by electrical transcription at Olympic Auditorium, Los Angeles, September 8, 1940, and at San Francisco, September 11, 1940.

III. THE SITUATION IN MEXICO

WORKERS and progressives in the United States would do well to watch events in Mexico with special attention, for they are intimately related to the developments within the United States and to the whole world situation. The armed uprising of the reactionaries, backed by the oil trust and American bankers as well as by Nazi forces, against which the Communists have warned for many months, seems to be coming into the open, into action, in the next weeks.

The Almazan counter-revolutionary camp, which threatens the Cardenas government and the constitutional succession of Manuel Avila Camacho with violent overthrow, represents basically those elements within Mexico—clericals, landlords, upper bourgeoisie—which have thrown themselves completely into the arms of foreign capital, principally the Wall Street interests, and to some extent German and British. It is a touching example of the international brotherhood of finance capital that these rival forces are able to unite around a single figure in Mexican politics, General Almazan, who openly organizes his uprising from New York and Brownsville, Texas.

Friends of Mexican independence and progress are very uneasy, due to most recent developments, about the manner in which the Cardenas government is meeting the reactionary threat. President Cardenas is trying to appease Wall Street, at the very moment that Wall Street's puppet announces a counter-revolutionary uprising from New York. He is setting his foot on a path similar to that followed by President Benes of Czechoslovakia a couple of years ago. We can but hope that the consequences for Mexico will not be of the same catastrophic nature. To prevent that is indeed a main task of the Mexican labor movement, and, as an advanced sector of that labor movement, the Communist Party of Mexico.

In this critical moment in Mexico's history, President Cardenas chooses to make slanderous public statements against the Union of Soviet Socialist Republics, in connection with the death of Trotsky at the hands of one of his own intimates. What motive could induce Cardenas to adopt this obvious and cheap Trotskyite slander? Clearly, it is a gesture of appeasement toward Wall Street and the Mexican reactionary camp. It has been hailed as such by the most vicious anti-Cardenas agitators in the United States press.

The Soviet Union has no cause to worry about such slanders, wherever they may come from. But the Mexican people have cause to worry, because they are the danger signals of a policy of appeasement of their worst enemies. American workers and progressives have cause to worry, for the fate of the Mexican labor movement and of Mexican independence is bound up with the cause of progress and peace for the United States. We can only be alarmed, when we see the signals of vacillation and appeasement in the leadership of the Mexican bourgeois-democratic national liberation movement. We know from international experience that the logical unfolding of such appeasement policy has always ended, when not reversed in time, in defeat and fascist enslavement for the masses of the people.

Great responsibility rests upon the Mexican labor movement, and upon the Mexican Communists, to strengthen all the forces of struggle and unity among the Mexican masses, to equip them with political clarity and understanding, to rouse and unite them against the Almazan counter-revolution, which represents foreign enslavement, and against all capitulation tendencies.

Daily Worker, *September 8, 1940.*

IV. TO THE MILLIONS WHO *ARE* AMERICA!

WE ARE witnessing a Presidential election campaign which is indeed a peculiar one. The issues and problems facing our country are fateful, of far-reaching importance, beyond anything in our national experience since the days of Abraham Lincoln. Yet the two major candidates, and their parties, are systematically blotting out every major difference between them on the most central issues. All possibility of choosing the future course of the United States, by casting ballots for one side or the other between Democratic and Republican parties, has been cut off from the voters, because both Mr. Roosevelt and Mr. Willkie stand for essentially the same policies.

A man from Mars visiting us now might jump to the conclusion that this fact is evidence of a peculiar unanimity of opinion, sentiment and interest among the 46,000,000 American voters. But certainly no intelligent American could make such a mistake. Not only is the divergence among the voters deeper and sharper than in many generations, but also, and more important, the decisive majority is opposed to the course toward militarization and war upon which Roosevelt and Willkie are united. But in order to find electoral expression for that majority opinion, the voters have no alternative but to break their traditional political allegiance, and turn to one of the minority parties, among which only the Communist Party offers a genuine alternative.

"HEADS I WIN, TAILS YOU LOSE"

There is no unity of the people in support of the united policy of Willkie-Roosevelt. But there is a new-found unity among our aristocracy of wealth and social position. The economic royalists, whose hatred was welcomed by the Roosevelt of 1936, are the very men who chose from their own top ranks the candidacy of Willkie, not to fight but to support the Roosevelt of 1940. Things have gone so far that one of the more candid and simple-minded Republican agitators, David Lawrence, uttered a cry of alarm the other day, and hysterically asked:

Why are business men so reticent in this campaign? Can anybody recall in recent weeks a single speech of importance by any outstanding industrialist or manager of any large enterprise urging the public to support Wendell Willkie? ... Of what are business men afraid?

Mr. Lawrence has, of course, missed the point of the whole affair. The business men are no longer afraid of Mr. Roosevelt, and that is the nub of the election campaign as it stands today. Mr. Lawrence is still living in the atmosphere of a dead and gone era, in which Roosevelt was threatening to "master" the economic royalists. Roosevelt long ago abandoned that fleeting ambition. He is now leading the "Battle of America" to "master" instead the labor movement and the majority of the American people. He is busily proving to the economic royalists that he is indeed "indispensable" for them and their imperialist ambitions. So the business men are not afraid of him. They are quite content to let the campaign run its course, knowing that whatever the outcome, they have their man. It is the old game of "heads I win, tails you lose." Tweedledum and Tweedledee were never so much alike as in 1940.

But the economic royalists are afraid—of the people. Even with the Presidential elections sewed up, they are afraid of the people. Even when Roosevelt can openly step outside the Constitution, on behalf of their class policy, and assume dictatorial powers in foreign policy, they remain afraid of the people. Even when conscription can be forced upon an unwilling people, for undefined imperialist aims, they are still afraid of the people. And that is why they even hesitate to speak up for the "barefoot boy of Wall Street" who comes right out of their own family circles.

They may well be afraid. This is 1940, not 1914 or 1917. Two and a half decades of experience with imperialist war and an imperialist peace of violence have taught the people much, and especially the working class. The people are developing a genius for undermining and defeating the best laid plans of the "upper classes," the real enemies of the people. The masses of the people may move slowly, but even when they only slightly stir, the economic royalists have learned to tremble.

The People Will Find a Way

Consider, for a moment, that un-American and unprecedented measure, the conscription law, that has been forced upon the country by the Willkie-Roosevelt coalition and the mobilized money power of the land. That was a heavy blow against the people, and a signal victory for Wall Street. Wherever our ruling circles gather about the festive board and spill champagne in celebration of this victory, there is a grinning skeleton at the feast to spoil their pleasure. They are haunted by the memory of a great labor movement of eight to nine million members, so consciously and unitedly against conscription that even the most trusted and reliable political agents of the Roosevelt-Willkie coalition, the men they draw into their "kitchen cabinets" and defense boards to "represent" labor, did not dare raise their voices in support of that measure, much as they desired, much as they were pressed to do so.

They are haunted by the fact that, in a Congress these gentlemen own body, soul and breeches, a Congress which has been registering their policies with all votes against one, when it came to the conscription bill and the people began to stir only a little, two-thirds of the Republican Congressmen voted against the measure which their Presidential candidate had endorsed, and its only solid support came from the Solid South where three-fourths of the people are disfranchised.

The significance of the vote against conscription in Congress is not diminished by the fact that the Republicans are equally reactionary with the Democrats, that they indulged themselves the luxury of this vote because they were assured of the bill passing anyway by Democratic votes, that they were guilty of the grossest opportunism and cynicism, that they were acting merely as the "Outs" giving a blow against the "Ins." All that is, on the whole, true, but it merely emphasizes another truth—that the Congressmen knew the people back home were so fiercely and consciously against conscription that it was "good politics," as the phrase goes, to go along with that sentiment. Yes, the fat boys have reason for sober second thought; in the imperialistic adventures they plan for America, the people will not remain for long mere passive pawns to be shoved around the chessboard of war.

Yes, in spite of the most gigantic conspiracy in American history to disfranchise the American people, to deprive them of a voice in the most fateful decisions our country has faced in many generations, the people find a way to make their voices heard and their influence felt.

A MOCKERY OF FREE ELECTIONS

That is why the economic royalists, the reactionaries who are hurrying America into a disastrous war, are afraid of the 1940 elections, despite the fact that they have the two major parties hog-tied and delivered before the event. That is why they are afraid of the Communist Party. Who knows, with the major candidates and parties united against a powerful swell of mass opinion and sentiment, that great numbers might not render their protest by voting Communist in November.

That is why the Roosevelt-Willkie united front forces are proceeding systematically to deprive the Communists of their political and electoral rights in this campaign. That is why they sent the West Virginia farmer, Oscar Wheeler, to prison for fifteen years, for a crime of soliciting signatures to a Communist election petition, on grounds of "false pretenses," although the petition was in pure legal form and no signer could have had the slightest doubt what he was signing. That is why in Illinois, the Kelly-Horner Roosevelt Democrats, on orders from Washington, staged mob violence against Communist election workers, and are holding dozens in jail on trumped-up charges of "sedition." That is why, in several states, high officials have openly defied the election laws to arbitrarily rule the Communist Party off the ballot. That is why, in New York, they are openly talking about finding some subterfuge to deny the Communists the right to have our ticket on the ballot, as we have had in every election since 1920.

The Roosevelt machine has an additional incentive to suppress the Communist Party. In Pennsylvania, Illinois, Ohio and especially in New York—all pivotal states—it is agreed that the vote may be so close that the Communists, even without any great increase in strength, might be the balance of power. The Roosevelt machine, thinking that the Communists cannot possibly vote for Wall Street's Willkie, hopes to steal our votes on behalf of Roosevelt by denying the opportunity to vote for our own candidate. In the past, the Roosevelt forces sometimes had our voluntary support, and in 1938 they held New York State against Dewey and the Republicans only with our help, by less than the margin of votes we threw to them. Now that they cannot get our voluntary support, they hope to obtain it by trickery and violation of free electoral rights. Wendell Willkie himself admitted, in an article in the *New Republic,* that the Roosevelt Administration's actions against the Communists, and specifically against myself, had this immoral and partisan motive—but that was before he became the Republican candidate, and even before his secret pact with Roosevelt! Now he will not break his silence on this issue, even to keep an important bloc of votes from being stolen for his rival, Roosevelt.

The truth is mighty; it is terribly embarrassing even to the most powerful political personages and combinations, although it be spoken only by the weakest of voices against which newspapers and radio have been conducting an unexampled campaign of slander and prejudice. That is why I cannot promise you that I will continue to speak to you throughout the campaign; the powers that be consider it more convenient to have me behind bars for the next several years. That is why I cannot promise you that you will have everywhere the opportunity to vote for the Communist ticket in November, for in many places our Party workers are being beaten up, or thrown into jail, or both, and our election petitions thrown out, their signers blacklisted and driven from their jobs.

And that is also why Candidate Roosevelt made a beautiful speech at Philadelphia the other day, extolling the virtues of free elections!

That is why, on the other hand, we firmly expect that among the millions of Americans, who truly believe in democracy, who truly believe in free elections, who truly hate conscription and war, who truly oppose our country being dragged into the bloody world scramble for empire with its profits for the few and starvation and death for the many—that among these millions who *are* America, a great number, greater than anyone now suspects, will vote Communist as the only way to vote in any degree as their own conscience dictates.

Speech delivered over the Blue Network of the National Broadcasting Company, September 25, 1940.

V. THE CHOICE BEFORE AMERICA'S YOUTH

TONIGHT, I wish to address myself especially to the young people of the United States, to those who have come to maturity during the period of the great crisis of the capitalist world now unfolding in the second imperialist world war.

You, young men and women, were born into the richest country in the world, a land whose wealth and productive powers were equal to all the rest of the world combined, where scientific technique was highest, where the current boast was that "prosperity" had become permanent. Even then, of course, half or more of the workers, young and old, had to console themselves with hopes for their failure to share in the "prosperity," but the dominant tone was unlimited optimism for the future. Before the present young generation had time, however, to begin to face their own problems of practical adjustment to life, the great crash of 1929-32 destroyed the illusions of the Coolidge-Hoover era. Since then, our young people have been groping for a new foundation upon which to build their expectations of life.

The false dawn of Roosevelt's New Deal period aroused great hopes and enthusiasms, especially in the younger generation. Then came the war, and with it the growing suspicion among the young people that Roosevelt was not dealing frankly with them, that under cover of fine phrases about neutrality and peace, he was actually taking us step by step into partisanship and final belligerency.

Last spring, the organized youth movement put the question squarely to the President when its delegates gathered in Washington for the Citizenship Institute. The President answered them with the one word, "twaddle." That word exploded the Roosevelt illusion.

A FOREIGN POLICY OF WAR

How sure were the instincts of the youth is now testified to by the unchallenged note, sounded from Washington one month before the national elections, that *"The United States may be at war by next spring, if not sooner."* It is testified to by the conscription law, which has sense and meaning only as preparation for plunging this country into the worldwide scramble for empire.

Conscription, militarization, and very soon a place in the very vortex of the imperialist world slaughter—these are the prospects held out to American youth by both Roosevelt and Willkie.

Last Wednesday in Cleveland, Mr. Willkie made some vote-catching gestures to the overwhelming anti-war sentiments of the American people. But every word he said about practical policy, about what to do *now,* was thought for thought and almost word for word, on the same line on which Roosevelt is not only talking but acting. If America is being dragged into the war, a fact now being generally recognized, it is precisely by the *present policies* upon which Willkie and Roosevelt are agreed—so closely agreed that Willkie quoted from Roosevelt's own words to express that agreement in his acceptance speech.

No, it is clear the American youth cannot express their deepest thoughts and feelings against the disastrous war into which they are being dragged by choosing between Willkie and Roosevelt.

Domestic policy has, for both Roosevelt and Willkie, been reduced to the position of "the tail that goes with the hide" of a foreign policy of war and preparations for war.

Consider for a moment the needs of American youth for education and jobs, which are harder and harder to obtain, and more and more precarious when gained. Out of years of bitter experience and profound thinking, the youth of America, through their broadest and most representative organizations, brought forth a program for a minimum satisfaction of their needs, that they might be en-

abled to marry, establish homes and become useful citizens. They
put this into the form of a practical legislative measure, called the
American Youth Act. They estimated that it would cost the Government about five hundred million dollars per year. They proved
that this would be the most remunerative investment that our
country could possibly make.

But Roosevelt has scrapped even his little beginnings in that
direction of the New Deal period, now long dead and gone. He
answered the young people who urged their plan upon him in
these words:

Don't seek or expect utopia overnight, don't seek or expect a panacea—
some wonderful new law that will give to everybody who needs it a
handout or a guarantee of permanent remunerative occupation of your
own choosing.

Those are the words, and express the thoughts of all the Willkies
of Wall Street who have fought with such bitter hatred against
every social and economic advance, even the smallest, that has
been wrung from them by the struggles of the people. Today,
Willkie and Roosevelt are united in telling the young people to
look to the army and to the munitions factories for all the solutions
of their problems.

Today it is the threat of war, of "national emergency," that is
used to justify this brutal and callous rejection of the demands of
the youth. But only a few months ago, before war and emergency
had been brought to our doorsteps by the Roosevelt-Willkie policies, they rejected the Youth Act with equal brutality; then they
said it would cost too much money, it would lead the country to
bankruptcy and ruin, America could not afford it.

How is it, you statesmen and gentlemen of the moneybags, that
a mere five hundred millions to educate the youth and train them
for useful work would in 1939 have threatened America with bankruptcy and ruin, while in 1940 you rush to appropriate fifteen billions, thirty times as much, for militarization and war, without a
single voice being raised from your midst to warn us that this is the

road to ruin? Either you were lying to us last year when you said our proposals for social expenditures were the road to disaster, or you are hiding from us this year the fact that you are rushing us on the road to disaster thirty times as fast. The truth is in both these alternatives: You were lying to us a year ago, and you are also rushing the country to catastrophe this year.

In this issue we find the explanation of why our economic royalists, the ruling class of America and their statesmen in and out of power, are rushing our country helter-skelter into the midst of the bloody world scramble for empire. Their system of rule, the system of capitalism, is rotting and dying; it is no longer working and cannot be made to work again so as to satisfy the needs of the people. So long as they cling to the capitalist system, they must fight for ever-rising profits for the big capitalists, the monopolists, the economic royalists. But big profits are eternally in opposition to the needs of the people, to rational expenditure of the national income for the people's needs. So they are driven, by the logic of their position, to sacrifice the people and to drive them into the world war, speculating to solve their insoluble problems at the expense of other peoples and other lands.

But war is no way out, it is only the hundredfold multiplication of all the ills of peace and the addition of new catastrophes.

THE FUTURE BELONGS TO THE YOUTH

The old order is dead. It can never be resurrected. Not Willkie nor ten thousand Willkies can take us back to the days of Coolidge and Hoover. Not Roosevelt nor ten thousand Roosevelts can restore life to a moribund economic and social system through the violence of war.

Young people, especially, are learning to understand that beyond all their immediate demands for the betterment of their present intolerable conditions, there is the deeper necessity to find a way out of the present mess to a new world.

There is no road back to the days of pre-war capitalism, to the old world. There is no by-path to any long-term compromise solution. There is, finally, only one road to the new world which youth is seeking. That is the road away from capitalism, to socialism. That is the road away from the rule of the capitalist class and toward the rule of the working class.

Capitalism is, and can only be, the ownership and control of the national economy, and everything that goes with it, by a small class of parasitical monopolists. That is the root of crises, unemployment, and all the social ills of mankind; it is the root of militarism and war.

Socialism is the only alternative to capitalism. It is the transfer of the national economy to the ownership and control of the entire people, incorporated into the working class, with the full utilization and development of the national economy for the benefit of all.

Socialism has been proved to be eminently practical. While the capitalist world is falling to pieces, the great socialist Soviet Union is forging ahead to prosperity, security and well being for two hundred millions of people. It is multiplying its national wealth at a rate unheard of in previous history, and distributing its benefits over the whole population. It is doing this in a hostile and warlike world, without assistance, and keeping itself out of the war through a powerful modern defense coupled with a vigilant and intelligent policy of good neighborly peace.

Not through Roosevelt nor Willkie, not through any party or policy that clings to the profit system and drives to war, can American youth find its way to the bright future world which they seek. Only the Communist Party points the way to the future. Only the Communists organize the workers to travel on that road. The future belongs to the youth—and to socialism.

Speech delivered over the Network of the Mutual Broadcasting Company, October 4, 1940.

VI. AN AMERICAN FOREIGN POLICY FOR PEACE

FOREIGN policy is a matter which deals with all the problems of war and peace. Our country is preoccupied today with the question of war. Yet there is almost complete absence of any serious discussion of foreign policy. In Congress wildly hysterical military appropriations are passed, one after another, that now mount up to fifteen billions of dollars, two-thirds of which no responsible person had the slightest idea was needed four months ago. This hysteria of appropriations was inaugurated by a message from the President, which solemnly recited the exact number of hours and minutes required to reach Omaha, Nebraska, and St. Louis, Missouri, by airplane from certain countries to the south. Candidate Willkie, on October 2, recorded the fact that he was "shocked" to learn the dangerous international position of the United States. He discoursed at length on his shock, but so far as policy is concerned, he said nothing new whatever, while he re-emphasized his agreement with the course on which Roosevelt has been and is taking our country. Like the President, like Congress, Mr. Willkie displays a naïve and childlike faith in dollars, expressed in military appropriations for machinery and implements of war, as the answer to all questions.

One and all, the leaders and ideologists of the Democratic and Republican parties alike forget one "little thing." They forget that armaments and soldiers are nothing but *instruments* of foreign policy, that *by themselves they answer no question whatever; that without an intelligent foreign policy armaments only multiply con-*

fusion and danger, that with a wrong-headed and dangerous foreign policy armaments only rush our country more quickly and deeply into disaster. And thus it is that every one in high places—and many in low—salves his conscience that he is doing everything needed to protect our country when he helps to pile one armaments appropriation upon another, when he votes for or agrees to register sixteen million young men for the draft, and when he roundly denounces any voice raising dissent, or calling for more fundamental consideration, as the voice of the unknown enemy, of the "Fifth Column."

I speak against this madness of armaments. I would use the fortunate circumstance that we are in the midst of national elections, that public discussion is not yet under the ban but only under serious attack, to put forward a serious examination of foreign policy.

First of all, glance at various European countries which have been conquered by the Nazi invaders during the past year. Seriously ask yourself the question: were they destroyed by lack of armaments or by a foreign policy which went contrary to their national interests? There can be only one answer: armaments were adequate if there had been intelligent foreign policy, but armaments turned out to be useless because of distorted foreign policy.

Take the Polish Government of Colonel Beck and the aristocrats and landlords of that country. Its foreign policy had been built upon relentless hostility toward its Eastern neighbor, the Soviet Union, and, since 1933, upon reliance upon Hitler Germany and participation with Hitler in crushing and dismembering weaker neighbors. The domestic counterpart of this foreign policy was one of brutal oppression of national minorities within its own borders which included 40 per cent of its total population, not to speak of the terrible exploitation of Polish peasants and workers. It had inflicted injuries upon every neighbor, so that all looked upon it with suspicion or open hostility. Its own subject population hoped for its downfall. When Hitler suddenly turned upon it with his demands, the Beck Government had no recourse but the paper guarantees of Mr. Chamberlain, and its armaments collapsed in thirty days.

The outstanding example, however, is that of France. There was the classical land of "military preparedness." Ever since the last war it had bankrupted itself with armaments, fortifications and militarization. Only seven years ago it was the undisputed mistress of the whole continent of Europe, west of the Soviet border. After Hitler's rearmament of Germany, France even obtained a mutual defense pact with the Soviet Union. France was in an unconquerable position. But, following a disastrous foreign policy, the French Government itself destroyed its own defenses one by one. It helped Hitler and Mussolini destroy the Spanish Republic; it betrayed Ethiopia; it sold out its ally, Czechoslovakia, at Munich; it tore up its mutual defense pact with the Soviet Union. When finally, at the bidding of Britain, the French Government declared war against Germany, it had already by its own foreign policy placed itself in the most disadvantageous position. And after it declared war, it *made* war not against Germany but against its own people, outlawing the French Communist Party and crushing the labor movement. Its enormous military machine was never even mobilized for action against the invaders. Most of its tanks were captured by Hitler, not at the front, but in the interior of France where they had been kept for use against the French workers. Of what use were armaments to France, when it followed such a foreign policy?

THE FOUNTAIN-HEAD OF DISASTER

Turn now for a look at the foreign policy of Great Britain. Here is to be found the source and fountain-head of most of the disasters of Europe and Asia and Africa, which have now climaxed with a month of daily air bombardments of London itself, and the horrible irony of British retaliation striking chiefly upon the quivering body of her ally of a few months ago, France. British foreign policy deliberately brought Hitler into power in Germany, and gave the chief, the indispensable, help for the German armaments that now strike at the British Isles. It was British foreign policy which deliberately scuttled the League of Nations; which abandoned China to the Japanese invaders; which determined the betrayal of Ethiopia, Austria, Czechoslovakia, Spain; which pressed France into tearing up its pact with the Soviet Union; which then pushed Poland, Norway, Holland and Belgium into a disastrous and hopeless war in which they quickly fell victims; which tried to create a desperate diversion in Finland; which led France to her collapse; which is now involving the United States in the general ruination. Of what use are armaments when they are in the service of such a foreign policy as that of Great Britain?

Did the British ruling class carry out this suicidal policy because they had deliberately decided to commit suicide? No, not at all. They were firmly convinced that it was a very, very clever policy which would end in giving them the world tied up in a nice bit of British red tape, without the necessity of firing a single British gun. The accumulated cunning and craft of centuries of rule, of the building of the empire upon which the sun never sets, went into the elaboration of that foreign policy. It was clever beyond description—far too clever, indeed, for it overreached itself.

There were two central thoughts dominating this clever British foreign policy: first, a Hitlerized Germany was to be encouraged and pushed into a war to destroy the Soviet Union, which would at the same time so weaken Germany as to remove her as a threat to Britain. Second, Britain's imperialist rivals were to be subordinated and made dependent upon Britain, in the case of France by the German threat, in the case of the United States by the threat of Japan, with perhaps warlike developments in each case in which Britain would act as the impartial judge and peacemaker. Thus would the blessings of the British Empire be spread over the face of the earth.

This super-clever foreign policy of Britain came to wreck on the rock of the Soviet Union. First, the Soviet Union had grown too strong and too consolidated to offer a tempting field for military adventures for a Hitler who likes to have his victories assured before he goes into action. Second, the leadership of the Soviet

Union was too wise and experienced to fall into the British trap. Both these factors are worthy of much more examination than we can take time for today, for the American people have been systematically taught, by newspapers and radio, to believe the Soviet Union to be very weak and its leadership to be stupid barbarians. Events of the past year should have been sufficient to dissolve such illusions!

Now, in the light of this analysis of British policy, turn to an examination of the foreign policy of the United States during the past ten years of world crisis. At every major point, American policy is found to be either an adaptation, or an outright copy, of the British "model." Limitation of time forbids the detailed listing of the well-known facts; but each of my listeners is fully capable of doing this for himself. The rulers of America have slavishly followed in the footsteps of their British cousins, with only such variations as were required by the special Anglo-American rivalries and antagonisms.

The foreign policy that has been developed by the United States Government over the past years, and which is now being pushed to its logical conclusions, has no promise for our country any better than that which it has already realized for the British. This policy is the common property of Roosevelt and Willkie, of the Democratic and Republican Parties, of nearly the whole American bourgeoisie. Only the Communist Party has proposed and consistently fought for a foreign policy of our country which could replace the disastrous policy now being followed.

A FOREIGN POLICY FOR PEACE

A clear-sighted and long-range foreign policy for the United States can only be developed upon the solid foundation of friendship and close collaboration between our country, China and the Soviet Union. That is now blocked by our shameful betrayal of China, through our supply to Japan, over the years, of the materials for her war of conquest, and by Washington's studied and artificial hostility toward the Soviet Union. Only when these features of our present foreign policy are wiped out can we begin to move toward a foreign policy which can guarantee peace and security to America.

Such a constellation of powers, the United States, China, and the Soviet Union, moving along agreed-upon lines fully consistent with the needs of the three great peoples, would be very powerful indeed. It would be a stable combination, for these countries have no rivalries or conflicting interests. It would be strategically powerful, because it would immediately hold the keys to three continents; a Washington-Moscow-Chungking Axis, solidly welded with correct policies, would be unmatchable in world politics. It would be physically strong, combining seven hundred to eight hundred millions of population, and the preponderance of the world's productive forces. It would be morally invincible, attracting the enthusiastic adherence of the suffering peoples all over the globe.

Some glimmerings of the bright light such a policy would bring to America and to the world shine through the remarks made in the House of Representatives in Washington by Congressman Sabath of Illinois on October 1. The key to Mr. Sabath's remarks can be seized in the following brief quotations. He said:

Yesterday's leading editorial in the *Washington Times-Herald* emphasizes a viewpoint concerning Russia that I have suggested and recommended on several occasions; the last time as recently as September 24. My query has been and still is today: Why should not the United States try to cultivate the good will of the Soviet Republics? It is realized now in many quarters that Great Britain made a serious if not well-nigh fatal mistake by not concluding and cementing friendly relations with Russia ahead of Germany. Should we repeat that error? ...

I know there are critics of Russia and its policies. Investigation will reveal, I sincerely believe, that a whole lot of the criticism of Russia is due to Nazi and fascist propaganda. That is one of the subtle tricks of the leaders of these two "isms." They conduct all kinds of subversive activities and then try to escape detection and blame by pointing their fingers at the Communists. ...

Regardless of what the Nazi, fascist, or capitalistic groups in the United States may say about Russia, I reiterate that the best interests of the United States will be served not by criticizing and assailing Russia

but by taking just the opposite course and seeking her friendly coopera-
tion. The latter course will inure to the benefit of America, and it is the
welfare and safety of America that in these critical days should be our
sole objective.

Those remarks contain a profound wisdom which Americans,
regardless of their opinion about socialism, would do well to ponder.

We Communists have been urging such a course upon our
Government for many years. But our words were dismissed as the
special pleading of a small minority who were interested mainly
in getting the United States to help the Soviet Union. Only now
is the true situation becoming clear to large numbers that the
Soviet Union is fully able to take care of herself without any outside help, that it is the United States that needs such a friend as
can be found only in the Soviet Union.

A word of warning is, however, in place at this point. It will be
worse than useless for the United States to approach the Soviet
Union in the hopes of finding an ally in a war, the aims of which
are to redistribute the colonies and subject peoples among the great
powers. The Soviet Union will never participate in such a war. It
will be equally futile and harmful for the United States to indulge
in such tricky maneuvering as Chamberlain carried on in Moscow
from June to August last year. And it will not be conducive to success of any attempt at rapprochement with the Soviet Union if it is
conducted by a government which is stamping out democracy at
home and establishing an American version of Hitlerism, for such
a government would have no moral advantage over a Hitler Germany and would be under a great geographical handicap.

I am no spokesman for the Soviet Union, and can make no
promises on her behalf. I am the spokesman for a growing body
of American workers and farmers, who see friendship and collaboration with the Soviet Union and China as the prerequisite for
a sound foreign policy for our country. We would wish to join our
efforts with all those of like mind to lead our country along such a
road as would make that not only possible but inevitable.

Only along such a road of foreign policy for America can our country win through, for itself and for the world, out of the present dangers and bloody chaos, into a new world of peace, order, and well being for all peoples in all lands.

SOME ASPECTS OF FOREIGN POLICY

THERE have been several requests that I deal with comments of the capitalist press on my Boston speech of October 6, and to develop further some of the points of that speech. I do this the more readily, since many persons have misinterpreted that speech to obscure one of its main points, which needs constant re-emphasis. I said:

It will be worse than useless for the United States to approach the Soviet Union in the hopes of finding an ally in a war, the aims of which are to redistribute the colonies and subject peoples among the great powers. The Soviet Union will never participate in such a war.

That would seem to be clear and definite. Yet for the capitalist press and commentators, another phrase was taken from the speech, and interpreted to mean just the opposite; namely, that I was advocating that the United States should seek to obtain the Soviet Union as an ally in the imperialist war. I must emphatically repudiate such a suggestion.

It is necessary for me, however, to admit that I carelessly helped these falsifiers, when I gave them the quotable and ambiguous formulation of a "Washington-Moscow-Chungking Axis" as a possible description of what would result from a correct people's policy for peace on the part of the United States. That made it too easy for gentlemen like Mr. Sokolsky and others to distort the whole question and obscure the real issues. Therefore I must disclaim this formulation of "Axis," and make this the occasion for deepening the whole question.

One of the chief features of the international situation, and the decisive factor for the United States, is the fact that the United States Government is pursuing a policy of feverish intervention in the imperialist war. It has embarked upon a gigantic and intense drive for building the greatest empire the world has ever seen, with the instrument of an overwhelming military machine. In this course it is expressing the will of the united American bourgeoisie. The policy and aspirations of Washington may be summed up in two headlines from *The United States News*—"Unofficial Merger of Britain and U. S." (Oct. 4, 1940), and "America to be Enriched by Vast British Holdings" (Nov. 29, 1940). For these aims American youth is conscripted, the masses are loaded with the burdens of enormous armaments, social and labor legislation is being dismantled, civil liberties are curtailed and swiftly being extinguished, and standards of living are driven down. For the masses the slogans are "national defense" and "democracy," but among the ruling classes it is frankly and outspokenly for "enrichment," for empire.

The American bourgeoisie is united behind this policy. But it is not fully united on *how to realize it*. One important difference is that one trend says, in the words of another headline in *The United States News,* that it would be wise to consider "Russia and China— New Allies for the U. S." (Oct. 11, 1940); or in the words of Drew Pearson and Robert S. Allen in a recent issue of *Look* magazine, "the U. S. and Russia are natural allies"; or to quote the *New York Daily News,* "We should hold our nose and make a deal with Stalin." Another trend says, in the words of George Sokolsky:

It is preferable to go down to defeat than to be victorious as the little ally of the Russian Brute. It is preferable to suffer the agonies of a prolonged world war than to accept peace as a bounty from Stalin. (*New York Sun,* Oct. 9, 1940.)

Now both these trends are part of the one war camp of the bourgeoisie. Both consider relations with the Soviet Union purely from the angle of whether the United States can or cannot use the Soviet Union as a catspaw for its own imperialist purposes. The first says it is possible and should be tried; the second says it is impossible and that to try it would be dangerous. Both are war policies, against the interests of the American working class and equally against the interests of the Soviet Union.

The American people, the real nation, are truly the "natural allies" of the Soviet Union and its peoples; but "Washington," that is, the present imperialist, war-making regime, is a natural enemy of the Soviet Union and of its policies of peace, of neutrality toward the imperialist war, of limiting the war and stopping it at the earliest possible moment. Washington, Roosevelt and the American bourgeoisie see in the Soviet Union the most powerful obstacle to the realization of their grandiose dreams of a far-flung American empire.

The approach of Washington and our ruling classes toward China is purely imperialistic. For years the United States complacently furnished the Japanese militarists with the materials for their war of conquest in China. Only now, when the Japanese threaten to seize the whole Far-Eastern colonial empire, including the rubber, tin, and oil of Indonesia, does the United States, still niggardly and half-heartedly, grant some credits to China and *threaten* to cut off supplies from Japan.

Clearly, under present circumstances, to speak of any alliance or even collaboration between the United States, China, and the Soviet Union, except as the result of the reversal or defeat of the present policies of Washington, only means to pour water on the mill of the imperialist war-makers.

Does this mean, however, that we shall not urge the American people to demand a correct policy toward both China and the Soviet Union, a policy that would truly be in the interests of the people of all three countries, a policy of peace? Of course, it means that we *shall* urge and fight for such a policy. But we must always point out that the people's interests clash with those of Wall Street, and the Wall Street-dominated government, and that such a policy must be imposed by the people.

Does this mean that the United States Government must inevitably, so long as it remains an imperialist, capitalist government, further follow up its hostile attitude toward the Soviet Union? Not necessarily, for even Nazi Germany found it advisable to replace its hostility with a formally correct attitude toward the Soviet Union. At least as much may be demanded, and gained, from the Government of the United States by an informed and alert working class.

Clearly, all phases of a correct people's policy of peace—neutrality toward the imperialist war, friendship with the Soviet Union, real help to China, the denial of aid to the Japanese invaders of China, limitation of the spread of the war, and its earliest end—all these things must be continuously demanded from whatever administration holds power in the country. They may be achieved in part by a sufficiently energetic struggle of the masses, against the will of the bourgeoisie, before imperialism is thrown out of power.

But they will be achieved only by struggle against the imperialist bourgeoisie and its policies, and never by falling under any illusions of collaboration between the working class and this imperialist bourgeoisie.

These considerations were the foundation of and were implicit in my Boston speech of October 6. Any contrary implications drawn from the "Axis" formulation are false and dangerous; and the use of that formulation is wrong as giving color to such implications.

The Soviet Union is the stronghold of peace for the workers and oppressed peoples of the world. It is fully capable of defending itself from any attacks, especially since it has the warm sympathy, love, and support of the toiling masses over the whole world. It is steadfastly holding its peoples outside the area of the imperialist war, giving an example thereby of how the interests of the American masses could best be protected. It is a beacon light showing us and the whole world the way out of capitalist oppression, starvation and war, to a new world of socialist freedom, plenty and peace.

An American Foreign Policy for Peace *was delivered by electrical transcription at Symphony Hall, Boston, October 6, 1940.* Some Aspects of Foreign Policy *was printed in* The Communist, *January, 1941.*

VII. THE AMERICAN WAY OF LIFE

WE HEAR a great deal about "the American way of life." Since we have been officially informed that it is to protect this "American way" that sixteen million of our boys must register for military service next week, and that fifteen billions of dollars have been appropriated this year for war preparations, it seems natural that we should inquire a little closer into just what is this "American way of life," anyway.

The American Bankers Association met in convention at Atlantic City not long ago, and also dedicated itself to the defense of the "American way of life." The bankers were a bit more specific than the President in defining just what they mean. They defined it as a way "based on free enterprise in a capitalistic economy." That is, we are being conscripted and are preparing a great military machine in order to keep our national economy in the hands of our small class of capitalists, by war if needed, and to keep these capitalists free of any serious interference. That is the basic thing about the so-called "American way of life," for which we are all of us supposed to be enthusiastically prepared to lay down our lives to preserve unchanged.

This "capitalistic economy" has indeed dominated America more and more since our establishment as a nation. It made the United States the "richest country in the world." But who has these riches? Is it the American people? Unfortunately, no. The mass of the people, those who do the work and produce the riches, have for generations been receiving proportionately less and less, and during the past ten years especially, have been receiving absolutely less and less. The rich are growing richer, the poor are growing poorer;

the number of the rich is constantly decreasing; the number of the poor is constantly increasing. The "American way of life," as the Bankers Association understands it, has put our country under the absolute control of a handful of monopoly capitalists.

The most astounding news item of a generation was revealed the other day—but practically suppressed by the newspapers. It was the investigation by a government body which revealed that effective control of United States economy lies in the hands of *three families*. Studying the two hundred largest corporations (excluding banks), which, in the words of the conservative Senator O'Mahoney, of Wyoming, "account for the bulk of activities in manufacturing, mining, electric and gas utilities, transportation and communication," the Senate Committee found, (1) that over half the stock is held by 75,000 individuals; (2) that a group of thirteen families, owning 8 per cent of the stock, occupy a decisive position of control over the whole; and (3) that in this group of thirteen families, more than half of the ownership and the most decisive control lies in the hands of three families, the du Ponts, the Mellons and the Rockefellers.

A few other official government statistical findings will round out this side of the picture: Among all corporations, the 5 per cent which are biggest own 77 per cent of the assets, and receive 86 per cent of the profits. Among this group, the very biggest, considerably less than 1 per cent of the total, represent more than half the assets and profits. Among all the banks of the country, 1 per cent hold 89 per cent of the resources.

Wealth Grows, Men Decay

And what is happening to our people? The National Resources Committee tells us the following: More than one million families have a yearly income below $250; 17 per cent of America's families and single individuals have an income of less than $500 per year, and more than one-fourth of them less than $750, while almost half of the population come under the bracket of less than $1,000 per year. This shows that the great majority receive far less than the

Government's own figure of the minimum required for an adequate livelihood. The famous but now forgotten "one-third of the population ill-housed, ill-fed and ill-clothed" must be revised to read two-thirds.

It was many years ago, long before these terrible contrasts had arisen, that a famous poet uttered a great truth, when he said:

> *Ill fares that land, to hastening ills a prey,*
> *Where wealth accumulates and men decay.*

The "American way of life," as defined by the American Bankers Association, has brought our country the greatest accumulation of wealth and the deepest decay of men ever seen in our history. Ten millions of unemployed, and a majority living below the level of decency, is matched at the top by a Brenda Frazier who blows in $35,000 in one night for a "coming-out party"; by a Barbara Hutton who spends millions of the Woolworth profits buying up stale European titles; by a Doris Duke Cromwell, who buys her playboy and ignoramus husband a nice Ambassadorship, and is now negotiating for a Senator's seat; by the "ten best-dressed women of America" who boast of spending a million dollars per year each on their clothes. This is the finest fruit of that "American way of life" which, in the classical words of the American Bankers Association, is "based on free enterprise in a capitalistic economy."

It is the bankers' definition of Americanism that guides both Democratic and Republican parties, both Roosevelt and Willkie. Both refer to Jefferson and Lincoln to justify their position, but both ignore the fact that monopoly has long ago wiped out "free enterprise" for the masses, based on free land and the frontier of a virgin continent, which for Jefferson and Lincoln was the basis of democracy, not the "capitalistic economy" of the Bankers Association.

Mr. Willkie, in defending his capitalist system in the speech at Pittsburgh last week, quoted at length from Lincoln's message to Congress of December, 1861. But he did not quote that part where Lincoln declared the foundation of "the American way of life," as he understood it to be, not the "capitalistic economy" of the Bankers Association, but that "large majority" of the people who "belong to neither class—neither work for others nor have others working for them." Lincoln, in that same address, warned that majority who were neither capitalists nor wage-workers to:

... beware of surrendering a political power which they already possess, and which, if surrendered, will surely be used to close the door of advancement against such as they, and to fix new disabilities and burdens upon them, till all of liberty shall be lost.

Similarly, Jefferson defined the "American way" in non-capitalist terms, in a letter to Adams in 1813, which said:

Here every one may have land to labor for himself, if he chooses; or, preferring the exercise of any other industry, may exact for it such compensation as not only to afford a comfortable subsistence, but wherewith to provide for a cessation of labor in old age.

And later, writing to a Mr. Spafford, in 1814, Jefferson said:

I fear nothing for our liberty from the assaults of force; but I have seen and felt much, and fear more from English books, English prejudices, English manners, and the apes, the dupes and designs among our professional crafts. When I look around me for security against these seductions, I find it in the widespread of our agricultural citizens, their independence and their power, if called on, to crush the Humists [the legalists of property-rights] of our cities and to maintain the principles which severed us from England.

Those foundations upon which Jefferson and Lincoln relied, of an agrarian democracy, of a population predominantly neither capitalists nor wage-workers, with such capital-labor relations as did exist tempered and modified by the free land of frontier—those foundations have entirely disappeared. Today, more than four-fifths of our population is entirely divorced from the land and depend, directly or indirectly, upon modern industry which is completely in the grip of monopoly. The population is predominantly composed of wage-workers, employed and unemployed, while almost all the non-wage-workers have completely lost the boasted independence of Jefferson's time, even the farmers becoming tenants or mortgaged to the banks or in the toils of the marketing monopolies. Free land has long disappeared, and the land is entirely monopolized; most workers can no longer exact anything near a "comfortable subsistence," while provisions for old age for the masses have become entirely a question of fighting for a governmental old-age pension system. The old economic foundation for democracy has been destroyed by the "capitalistic economy" which has developed into monopoly.

Unless a new economic foundation is found, democracy, already sick unto death from malnutrition, will surely die. But such a new economic foundation can be found only by limiting, modifying, and finally abolishing that capitalistic economy and the system of rule raised by it. To be free, the people must own and control their own economy, but in this age of modern, large-scale industry, they can own their own economy, not through individual private ownership, but only through collective public ownership.

The task of finding a solution to this problem can no longer be postponed. Monopoly capitalism has already reached the point in its development at which either it will crush the people or the people must abolish it and find new safeguards to their welfare and security, a new system of economy and of government.

CAPITALISM IN DECAY

That very bankers' convention which, the other day, sang the praises of "the American way of life based on a capitalistic economy," in the same document made admissions which damn that system beyond all salvation. It summed up the results of this system for the past ten years in these words:

For the first time in our history the production of American industry has made no net gains for a full decade. Industrial output has stagnated. Much of our factory equipment, and that of our transportation system, has become obsolete or obsolescent. For the first time our national standard of living has declined.

Our present economic system is obviously declining, decaying. Yet both major political parties, both Willkie and Roosevelt, reject any serious efforts even to bolster it up from within, as, for example, with a fifteen billion dollar governmental appropriation to produce more food, clothing and housing for the broad population; such a measure, they claim, would break down and destroy "the American way of life" as they understand it. But they are agreed that fifeeen billions of dollars, spent for engines of destruction, for war, is necessary precisely in order to "defend the American way of life." Those who taught us over many years that huge expenditures, even for production of the needs of life, was the road to ruin for our nation now rush us without debate into greater expenditures for war—and they call it "national defense."

Not war, nor preparations for war, can cure or in any way alleviate the sickness of the capitalist system from which we, together with the whole world, are suffering. It is from this sickness, from this crisis of capitalism, that the war has arisen. The war will only multiply all the ills of our present society a hundredfold. It was capitalism, with its inner contradictions, its sickness, its crisis, which brought on the last world war. It was capitalism which gave us the so-called peace of 1919, a peace of violence and oppression leading directly to the present war. It was capitalism which gave birth to Hitler and Mussolini and to the militarist imperialism of Japan, and which is now reducing to their level all the other capitalist lands, including our own. There is no way out, for America or for the world, which does not start with a sharp fight, not for the defense of "capitalistic economy," but for its fundamental change, for a new system to take its place.

SOCIALISM THE ONLY WAY

Socialism, the common ownership and operation of the national economy by and for all the people who toil, is the only alternative to capitalism. It is the only way the American way of life, as understood by Jefferson and Lincoln, can be preserved. Socialism is not a mere theory untested in life. It has been tried out with magnificent success in a great land, the Soviet Union.

American newspapers, radio and pulpit, together with the Norman Thomas Socialists, join in telling the American people the most horrible stories about the Soviet Union, striving mightily to convince them that the Soviet Union is the worst place on the globe. But if their stories are true, how is it that the Soviet Union emerges more and more as a great power in the world, growing stronger while other nations grow weaker? If their stories are true, how does it come that the Soviet economy multiplies tenfold its production of wealth for the people, during the same period in which the Bankers Association tells us that American economy has "stagnated"? If their stories are true, how is it that the Soviet Union has maintained peace for itself, while the rest of the world plunges madly into the most bloody and destructive war? If their stories are true, why is it that the Soviet Union, standing alone among the governments of the world, gives its people a profound and calm confidence in its security and its future, while all the rest of the world, including the United States, undergoes a hysteria of fear and feels nothing but doubt for the future? These facts are all unquestionable, and they give the lie to the horror-tales spread against the Land of Socialism, the Soviet Union. We have much to learn and many benefits to gain from the Soviet Union. The founders of America were not afraid to learn from other lands. "By their fruits ye shall know them!"

In this 1940 election campaign, only the Communist Party comes to the people with a clear explanation of the cause for our present ills, which are destroying the best traditions of the American way, a platform of immediate measures for their alleviation and a program for the future which will fundamentally solve our problems.

The Communist Party is educating and uniting the working people to fight for peace, for a better life and for security for all. That is why the servants of Wall Street try to suppress and outlaw us. That is why millions of Americans are coming to our defense, learning to trust and follow us. That is why the Communist Party has emerged as a major factor in the 1940 elections.

Speech delivered by electrical transcription in Detroit, Milwaukee, and Chicago, October 11-13, 1940.

VIII. A TRIBUTE TO JOHN REED

JOHN REED won immortality by his report of the first socialist revolution, the founding of the Soviet power, in the *Ten Days That Shook the World*.

It is not the peerless and inspired reporter, however, but the partisan of a cause who won the heart of his generation and whose name came to symbolize the movement of the best representatives of the American intellectual world, in their break away from the old decaying world order, their espousal of the new socialist order. It is in the role of passionate partisan of socialism, of the struggle for socialism, that the memory of John Reed waxes with the passing years. He was a great pioneer on the frontier between the old and the new social systems, the death struggle between which dominates our era.

An understanding, penetrating study of Reed's life, which would bring out in bold relief his lasting significance as an historical figure has still to be written.

Born and bred in the tradition of the privileged classes, Reed had further the advantage of talent and personality to open for him the doors of all the bourgeois world has to offer. But long before he was conscious of it, he was in revolt against the inner emptiness of that world. More and more he became a seeker for something unknown, something to fill the emptiness which his world, with all its education and experience, had left in him.

Reed found what he was seeking in Petrograd, Russia, in the days of October and November of 1917, when the Soviet Government was established, when the first Socialist Revolution began. He found it in the Party of Lenin, the Bolsheviks, the Communists, which guided that revolution.

From the revolution and the Party of Lenin which guided it, Reed acquired a faith and an understanding which gave meaning and dignity to life, which transformed the seeking adolescent into a whole man. He immediately identified himself wholly with the revolution, with socialism, with the Party of Lenin. He became the passionate partisan of a great cause. He had found himself in something so big that in it he could completely lose himself, merge himself. He had found the road away from decay and death, toward growth and life; away from the old life that had poisoned him and his generation, into the new life of affirmation, of belief, of unlimited perspective, of the future.

That experience which John Reed shared with only a minority of his generation of Americans is the experience through which the whole generation of today is now going.

Once again, as in John Reed's day, the decaying capitalist order, the bourgeois world, has been thrown into the violent paroxysm of imperialist war. Once more a whole generation of youth is called upon to offer its lifeblood in a war without aims beyond the indefinite repetition of the past which produced this war. Once more the recruiting sergeants and conscription boards call youth to the colors to fight—for the preservation of the dead past.

Today, however, the young generation stands on the shoulders of the generation of John Reed. He could only see the birth of the new order of socialism; the present generation celebrates the glorious achievements of twenty-three years of Soviet power. He had time only for the intuitive grasp of the great vision of Lenin; the present generation has deeply absorbed the teachings and examples of Lenin's giant successor, Stalin.

In John Reed's day, the American bourgeoisie was arrogantly confident of its power, of its hold on the young generation; today, the bourgeoisie is filled with a dark fear, it is vaguely conscious of its approaching doom, it knows it has lost its hold upon the youth, it struggles desperately to win the young generation again, with the blood of youth to rejuvenate itself.

The other day I thought of John Reed as I was reading a speech, directed toward American youth, by the most talented fugleman of the moribund old order, Archibald MacLeish. Beating the drums of war, this Laureate of Death was forced to admit, in order to combat, the deep disillusionment of the younger generation with the social order of present-day America. He identified this social order with democracy, and said:

We are wondering whether democracy in the United States has other spiritual weapons than the doubts and misgivings which ten years of depression and twenty years of skepticism provided for the men of France to fight with.

To provide those missing "spiritual weapons," MacLeish with great eloquence invokes the spirit of the Americans of "the thirties and forties of the last century," men "who had no questions about themselves." He describes them:

The smartest, toughest, luckiest, leanest, all-around knowingest nation on God's green earth. Their way of living was the handsomest way of living human beings had ever hit. Their institutions were the institutions history had been waiting for. If you had told them anyone else had a harder hold on the earth than they did, or anyone else believed in himself more than they believed in themselves, they would have laughed in your face.

And MacLeish calls upon the present skeptical and doubting generations to gaze upon his attractive picture of the past in order to imitate their more virile forebears.

Then MacLeish says a few words which, unconsciously, betray the emptiness of his whole eloquent appeal:

That was the way it used to be in this country. That was the way it was while the people of this country were clearing the quarter-sections for a free man's fields.

Your capitalist order, Mr. MacLeish, has abolished the "free man's fields," and with them the America whose glories you sing as a war song for the present generation. In their place are the crowded and regimented cities, the great factories of mass production and super-exploitation of labor, the F.B.I. of Mr. Hoover, the labor-spy agencies, the outlawing of minority parties, book-burnings and imprisonment for possession of books, draft boards, finger printing and registrations, unemployment, the petty persecutions of W.P.A. and relief bureaucrats. Restore the "free man's fields," Mr. MacLeish, and then perhaps your nostalgic dream-Americans will rise to your exhortations!

I wonder if Mr. MacLeish ever, in the dark hours of sleepless nights, ponders over the significance of this fact, that while his poetic description of the Americans of a century-gone is widely at variance with the Americans of today, yet there are peoples to whom his words could be currently applied with full accuracy. But only in one particular area of the world. Only in the Soviet Union, among the people whose mastery of life arose from new institutions, which "history had been waiting for," socialist institutions, whose rise was chronicled by John Reed in 1917, whose cause John Reed espoused as the forerunner for the present generation.

John Reed has been dead now these twenty years. But his spirit lives today in millions of young Americans. It is a thousand times more virile than that of the MacLeishes who call upon the glories of the past in order to drape the hideous, rotting features of the present, to entice the hungry and seeking young generation into the bloody crusade to save a capitalism that has become Monopoly and Death. The MacLeishes can never restore faith, enthusiasm, passion, wholeness, to the American youth. These things they will find only as they follow the tradition and example of John Reed. And that is the destined road for our America.

Speech delivered at John Reed Memorial Meeting, October 20, 1940.

IX. THE FIGHT FOR THE BALLOT

Abridged testimony of Earl Browder before the Senate Committee Investigating Fraudulent Election Practices, Senator Guy M. Gillette, chairman, Washington, D. C., October 25, 1940.

THE CHAIRMAN: At this time, the Committee has been requested to hear Mr. Earl Browder and I don't know whether he has additional people with him. Are you Mr. Browder?

Mr. Browder: Yes, sir.

The Chairman: Mr. Browder, if you will come over here, we will be very glad to hear any matter that you wish to present to us. Your full name is what?

Mr. Browder: Earl Browder. Earl Russell Browder.

The Chairman: And you reside where?

Mr. Browder: At 7 Highland Place, Yonkers.

The Chairman: You are a candidate for election to the Presidency?

Mr. Browder: I am the candidate for the Presidency of the Communist Party of the United States.

The Chairman: Mr. Browder, you made the request, I believe, or someone for you, for an opportunity to appear before this Committee, and present some matters that you wished to direct our attention to.

We are glad to have you and we are glad to listen to any matter that you wish to present to us. You may do so in your own way, in your own manner.

Mr. Browder: Thank you, Senator Gillette.

The Chairman: Proceed.

Mr. Browder: I appreciate very much this opportunity and I will be as brief as possible in spite of the voluminous character of the material that I have to deal with.

The Chairman: Might I interrupt you there long enough to say, Mr. Browder, that we want to keep the record as small as we can.

Mr. Browder: I appreciate that.

The Chairman: The funds that we have to use are limited.

Mr. Browder: Yes.

The Chairman: And these people are very heavy in their charges.

Mr. Browder: I appreciate that.

The Chairman: So we don't want to put anything in the record that we can avoid.

Mr. Browder: I appreciate that, Senator, and as much as possible I will place material at the disposal of the Committee as supporting material.

The Chairman: That would be preferable.

Mr. Browder: Yes.

I am placing before this Committee evidence of wholesale and organized corruption, fraud, intimidation and violence directed toward influencing and determining the Presidential election results, in violation of the Hatch Act, the Corrupt Practices Act, of the Constitutional safeguards to free elections, as well as embracing a series of violations of criminal laws.

The material I am submitting might thus deserve the attention of any instance of legislative, executive or juridical authority, charged with the responsibility for orderly public life, but it seems particularly within the scope of this Committee because it is organically bound up with the whole complexion of the 1940 elections in the degree of freedom under which these elections will take place.

My party has practically exhausted every avenue of appeal for redress of those grievances directly appertaining to us, which I will set forth, before coming to this Committee.

In some instances, our appeals have been upheld by courageous and incorruptible public servants and we are more than glad to record such facts, giving credit where credit is due, but, unfortunately, these instances are the exception, not the rule.

In general, we must record a wave of lawless and brazen overriding of every legal safeguard of free elections before which public officials of all grades are bowing, or in which they actively participate.

We are not here merely to complain of violations of the civil rights of individuals or minority groups; we are dealing with the purity of the electoral process itself, of the unshadowed authenticity of the final election results which is threatened by the developments we place before you.

These facts, at the least, require a record for history, even if it should prove impossible in these troubled and chaotic times to find immediate remedies, although we hope that there may be some immediate remedy found.

I want, first of all, to speak about the situation in New York State and to give my major attention to that, although we have a series of states in which even more flagrant violations of law have occurred, but which are not of such general interest as those in New York.

The Communist Party in New York State has been, by judicial decision, removed from the ballot after having been certified by the Secretary of the State.

The Chairman: What judicial body rendered that decision?

Mr. Browder: A judge of the Superior Court, I believe, by the name of Murray—I do not know his exact status—Justice of the Supreme Court, William H. Murray, hearing a petition brought by two members of the American Legion, asking that the Party be taken off the ballot because of insufficiency of signatures to its petitions.

The Chairman: And the decision was based on the support that was shown for that allegation of insufficiency of signatures?

Mr. Browder: That is right.

The Chairman: All right, proceed, Mr. Browder.

Mr. Browder: We have attempted to get before this Judge the facts, which we will call to your attention here, but without success.

I do not want to attempt to pass upon the technical legal questions involved, of the admissibility of evidence, but clearly there is a much larger scope for seeing and examining all sides of such questions before a legislative committee than there is before a court, and, surely, here I will not be subjected to the same limitations.

I first want to call your attention to the fact that the attack upon these petitions of the Communist Party in New York State in no wise attacked the authenticity of the signatures. Every signature that was registered—some 43,000 or more—is admittedly authentic.

Petition Signers Intimidated

The attacks upon the sufficiency of the number is directed toward that which says there must be at least fifty in each county, and those who are interested in removing the Communist Party from the ballot selected two counties and attempted to prove that the signatures, although they were actually given by registered voters, were obtained under false representation; and there were brought before the Court some 160 out of 200 signers, who were placed on the stand to state that they did not know what they were signing, and, therefore, wished to have their names removed.

Each one admitted that he had signed the document—it was his signature. Each one said that he did not know what he was signing and, therefore, wanted his signature removed. Aside from the legal question involved as to whether there is such a thing as a withdrawal of signatures once placed on a public document, the main point that I want to establish here is that these so-called withdrawals of signatures were, themselves, the result of and evidence of fraud, misrepresentation and intimidation.

Clearly, these people had been intimidated and brought into court to testify as they did under threat of the loss of their livelihood.

The Chairman: Was that question of intimidation or coercion raised in the hearing of the court?

Mr. Browder: It was, and I will present to you evidence sustaining this charge, which was not admitted into Court because the Court insisted that such evidence could be admitted only as it related to those two counties, and they attacked our petitions only in the counties where we were not able to get the direct evidence of that intimidation, and where we could not force this issue upon the victims of this intimidation because we had no way of protecting them.

We could no more get evidence of the intimidation in Greene County, New York, than one could get evidence of an intimidation in a Hitler election in Germany, but we can give you plenty of surrounding evidence which was excluded by the Court, which will be convincing, I believe. And, if that should not be sufficient, I would urgently request that if it were possible for someone such as yourselves—representing an authoritative body, who could give the people the assurance that what they say would not bring upon them victimization—to go into Greene County, he could in one day secure sufficient evidence of this intimidation to convince anyone.

If you should go into Greene County tomorrow and interview fifteen or twenty of those 160 people, taking them at random, under conditions which guaranteed that they could not be immediately identified and further victimized, and take their testimony in private with the assurance that they have nothing to fear of further trouble—which is the great cry they all raise—"We want no further trouble," they say; "we have already had too much trouble; our lives are being disorganized; we are being driven out of our community; we are losing our jobs; we are being taken off relief; we can't stand it"—and if you do reach these people with the assurance that this would not be further intensified, they would tell you the truth.

VOTES THAT DON'T BELONG TO THEM

Now, why has this campaign been made to take the Communist Party off the ballot? We are a small minority party there. It is clear to everyone that we have no chance of sweeping the State and electing our candidates.

Why, therefore, do people consider it sufficiently important to spend large sums of money and engage great organizations in the systematic hounding of people who sign our petitions, until, in desperation, they go before courts and withdraw their signatures?

It is because in New York State this question is not merely an example of the general persecution of the Communists that is sweeping over the country, in which Democrats and Republicans, alike, are engaged—in New York State this is a special project of the Democratic Party organization for the purpose of securing an advantage in the election over the Republican Party.

They want, by keeping the Communist Party off the ballot in New York, to secure for the Democratic ticket the votes which would be cast for our ticket.

This becomes important because it is generally agreed that in New York State, the balance of forces between the two major parties is very even, and that even a small number of votes might be the balance of power, throwing it one way or the other.

The Chairman: What is the basis for that assumption, Mr. Browder, that these votes that would otherwise be cast for the Communist ticket in New York would be cast for the Democratic Party?

Mr. Browder: The basis of that assumption is that it has so occurred in the past and, in the 1938 elections it was precisely the votes of the Communists which were decisive in the gubernatorial election.

The Chairman: May I interrupt you there? Don't you think that that is a rather unjustified conclusion? There is no way that you or I have of determining how these men voted except their own statements.

Mr. Browder: No, but politics is based upon certain assumptions and while one cannot give scientific evidence to prove them, the very fact that these assumptions exist become political motives, and in New York it has been assumed and so stated in the newspapers that the assumption was—I will be glad to furnish you with those documents—the assumption was that if the Communist Party was not on the ticket, the votes, which would otherwise go to the Communists, would be impossible of being thrown to Willkie and, therefore, would go to Mr. Roosevelt.

The Chairman: But after all, Mr. Browder, it is no more than an assumption, a statement of opinion of someone who has deduced that, is it not?

Mr. Browder: Yes, and I am only bringing this forward as an assumption and to point out that this assumption is based upon the experience of the 1938 elections.

This experience of the 1938 elections is also the explanation of why we had to get petitions to place the Party on the ballot. The Communist Party is strongest in New York State and in 1938 cast some 106,000 votes. That is our strongest place.

Under the State Laws, 50,000 votes for a party is enough to give it a place on the ballot without petitions, but this applies only on the vote for Governor and not for any other office; but it so happens that in 1938, the Communist Party withdrew its candidate for Governor out of deference to the American Labor Party with which we were trying to co-operate, and which was supporting the candidacy of Lehman.

Our vote was cast on a statewide scale only for the candidate for Congressman-at-Large. Our candidate was Mr. Amter, who got 106,000 votes, which, if also cast for a candidate for Governor, would have placed us permanently on the ballot. But because we withdrew our candidate for Governor in favor of the American Labor Party candidate, Mr. Lehman, we lost our place on the ballot.

Mr. Lehman won that election by 64,000 votes. If it had not been for the Communist Party withdrawing its candidacy and taking the extra burden that fell upon us in regard to that account, Mr. Lehman would have lost and Mr. Dewey would have been elected.

This is a fact which is a matter of record open to anyone's investigation who wants to verify it. It does not depend on anyone's assumption; and upon that fact, the assumption has been made by the machine leaders of the Democratic Party in New York State that if they could remove us from the ballot they could force us to give that co-operation which in 1938 we gave voluntarily; and that is the motive—the special motive beside the general motive that cuts across party lines—behind the attempt to get rid of the Communist Party from elections generally. That is the special motive which has created the situation where we have been, as I say, denied our place on the ballot in spite of the fact that we have complied with the law four times over in respect to signatures to our petitions, in such a way that every signature was so carefully guarded. I do not think there was ever a nominating petition of any large scale filed in any state in the Union which was so pure in respect to the safeguards that were placed around the collection of each and every name.

As to the charges that we were guilty of fraud and misrepresentation in the collection of these signatures, let me point out how impossible that would be. Here is the petition which was signed. Anyone looking at the petition cannot fail to know what he is signing. At the top in large letters is "Communist Party," the candidates in large letters, Earl Browder and James W. Ford. It is impossible for anyone to sign such a document without being fully cognizant of what he was doing.

They did not know that exercising their right to sign such documents would subject them to the persecution which followed.

Storm Troop Tactics

Now, I would like to cite you some evidence which shows how they terrorized these people. In the first place, they involved the W.P.A. and its administrative officers to lay the foundation for the terrorization.

A statement was issued by Lester Herzog, the up-state administrator of W.P.A., in which he announced that he was going to make a careful inspection of the Communist election petition and that those who signed the petition, if they knew what they were signing, would be fired from their jobs.

This was followed then by a campaign by people who claimed they represented the American Legion. I do not like to believe that their claim is correct.

The Chairman: Before you pass to the statement to which you referred of Mr. Herzog, were you reading from a newspaper clipping or were you making that statement yourself?

Mr. Browder: I was reading from a newspaper clipping which I will give you for the evidence. This is from *The New York Times.*

The Chairman: It is unnecessary to give it for the evidence. I am wondering if there is any basis for the statement that Mr. Herzog made excepting the newspaper report.

Mr. Browder: It was printed in the *Knickerbocker Press* in Albany on several days repeatedly in a prominent place. It was not merely printed once; it was printed for four or five days consecutively. It was never denied by Mr. Herzog and the facts are that Mr. Herzog and others under his direction did call on signers of the petition.

The Chairman: What was the name again, please?

Mr. Browder: Up-state New York Administrator of Works Project Administration.

The Chairman: And these statements were alleged to have been made when?

Mr. Browder: Immediately after the filing of the Communist petition in Albany. This clipping here is dated October 12 from Albany and on that date and succeeding days in Albany, the *Knickerbocker Press* carried in a prominent place the same statement.

In those days immediately following, people calling themselves the American Legion began systematically to call upon or to send communications to every signer of the petition.

Here is a postcard sent to Ethel Johnson, 95 Herchner Street, Albany, mimeographed:

The American Legion in Albany County has learned that your name is on a petition circulated by the Communist Party for the purpose of placing the Communist Party on the ballot of this election. We know many of the signatures are not valid. If this is true in your case, you may repudiate your signature if you will come to the rooms of the Capital City Post, 81 Columbia Street, Albany, before 8 o'clock Tuesday night. The rooms will be open from noon to 8 P.M. Tuesday. The Legion is giving you this chance to contradict the people who have deceived you.

Then committees called upon each one of these people. We do not have authentic documentary evidence from Greene County of what the committees did and what they said. Here the terrorization was so complete that we could not get one person who dared to break through.

The Chairman: Is Greene County an up-state county?

Mr. Browder: Yes, the county seat is Catskill, thirty-five miles from Albany, but from surrounding counties we have statements from people who were called upon by the American Legion and who did sign the documents.

Here is one from Brushton, New York, answering a letter sent out by the Communist Party. By the way, I should remark here that immediately after the collection of these signatures the Communist Party sent out a letter addressed to each person who signed the petition thanking him for his support in getting on the ballot.

In the testimony in the Greene County hearing, each one who came on the stand was asked whether he had received such a letter.

The Chairman: Let me interrupt you again. When you speak of the Greene County hearing, was that the hearing that Judge Murray finally ruled on?

Mr. Browder: Yes, Judge Murray presided. It was adjourned for the purpose of saving the 160 people this trip to Albany.

The Chairman: I see.

Mr. Browder: Each one of those 160 people who was placed on the stand there was asked if he had received such a letter from the Communist Party and each one answered, "I didn't read it. I threw it into the stove." Although the letters were mailed in a plain envelope, and even if they had been warned before that they should not read anything that came from the Communist Party, they would not have known it came from the Communist Party unless they had opened it. Each witness gave uniform testimony on this point: that he did not read a letter from the Communist Party because he threw it into the stove. Now, here is some data from some people outside of Greene County. Here is a letter from Frank Duby, Brushton, New York, answering a letter:

Dear People: Just received your letter of the 13th. Do not know what to think of it. I will give you a little insight as to what I was told Sunday. They came to the house with the papers I signed. Told me I should not have put my name on it. I draw old-age pension and they would take it away and I would lose my citizenship and we would be put in detention camps until after the war. This was a hard thing to put up to us as there are three or four hundred in this county who put their names on the paper and they said the men that were here were in jail now. If any more information you wish, send a man. I will help him to investigate the matter. You can size this up and I will help. (Signed) Frank Duby.

Another letter: Marianna Costello—this does not have the town marked on it, but I can get it if you wish.

I am not a member of the Communist Party. I have never been a Communist. I am a good American. I go to church three times a week. I believe in the Bible and all its teachings. We have accepted the Lord Jesus as our personal Savior. When I signed the Independent Nominating Petition, the man who collected my signature told me it would be absolutely legal to sign, and that it was nothing bad. I do not wish to be caused any trouble or involved in any dispute or unpleasant circumstances because of my signature. I also signed a statement for the American Legion when they told me that I was registered as a member of the Communist Party when I signed their Nominating Petition.

Another letter from Frank Hobbs, 96 Orange St.; again the town is missing but I will submit it later.

I took my name off the Communist petition because the American Legionnaires told me I did something against the Government and I was afraid.

I want my name back on the Communist petition because I believe they have a right to be on the ballot.

I am not a member of the Communist Party but believe in upholding the rights of the colored race.

Another one, James W. Payne, 89 Orange St., Albany, Oct. 16. 1940.

I, James W. Payne, knew what I was signing when I signed the Communist petition.

I withdrew my name when I was told by the American Legionnaires that I was harming America.

I still want my name on the Communist petition because I believe they should be on the ballot.

From Carmine Ferrucci, Amsterdam, New York.

I am not a member of the Communist Party and I don't want to become one. But I knew that I was signing a petition to put the Communist Party on the ballot.

From Theodore Davis, Amsterdam.

I knew that I signed the petition to put the Communist Party on the ballot and I agree to keep it there.

From George Wright, Amsterdam.

I know that I signed the petition to put the Communist Party on the ballot. When two men came to ask me to take my name off, I refused to do this—

The Chairman: Were these letters that you are reading from the letters of the 160 who withdrew their names or threw their letters in the stove?

Mr. Browder: No, in Greene County we could not get statements. They concentrated on Greene County. They decided that was our weakest point and they concentrated there. We could get these letters outside of Greene County, because their forces were concentrated in Greene County.

The Chairman: Mr. Browder, the additional statements are along the same line as you have just read?

Mr. Browder: Yes.

The Chairman: Then to prevent the record from being encumbered too much, will you file them?

Mr. Browder: Yes.

The Chairman: If you wish to, leave them with the committee.

Mr. Browder: I will leave a selected number. I won't insist on putting all of these in the record. I know it would encumber it. In correcting the record, I would like to place some in the record. I will go over these later and pick out the most typical and representative.

Now, I want to point out that the attack upon the signers, especially in Greene County, took the form, almost in every case, of telling them that by signing the petition they had joined the Communist Party and thereby made themselves subject to loss of jobs, loss of pensions, loss of rights, even the possibility of being thrown into concentration camps. And the document which they asked them to sign to repudiate this, they told them, was a form of resignation from the Communist Party. This is established in the records of the Court. This is something that we did get into the record, although very much was excluded, and there the record is the *prima facie* evidence that the repudiation of signatures was secured by false representation.

The theory of fraud was based upon the assumption that we did not tell these people that they were joining the Communist Party when they signed this petition. The theory was that we did not warn these people that by signing the petition they were losing their rights; and, therefore, it was misrepresentation.

The Secret Behind the Attack

Now, I want to give some evidence to show why this campaign was considered of such importance that all of these forces were thrown behind it to achieve this result. I know that newspapers are not good evidence in court, but I do not know of any other evidence which can indicate what is going on in the minds of leaders of political movements except the newspapers and their reports.

Therefore, I want to call your attention to the *New York World-Telegram,* by no means a Communist paper or in any way sympathetic to our cause, which has itself supported, for many years, every effort to keep us off the ballot. In its issue of Saturday, September 7—I have these quotations in a written form here which will save me the trouble of going through the paper, but I will offer you this paper in support of the evidence.

On September 7, on page 3, a political writer reviewing the election situation in the State of New York, under an eight-column headline: "Loss of American Labor Party Left Wing Votes Carries Threat to Roosevelt in State," concludes a long examination of the state situation with the following words:

It constitutes a threat to the President's ability to rally the radical vote to his standard so long as Earl Browder, Communist, has his name on the ballot. The loss of any considerable number of radicals, who virtually unanimously supported him four years ago, would be inimical to his chances of carrying the state. . . . It is admitted . . . the loss of 100,000 votes . . . may prove enough to lose the state. . . . Browder must be nominated by petition, which must have 12,000 signatures, and at least 50 from each county in the state. . . . It is a safe surmise that the Democrats and the A.L.P. conservatives will scrutinize carefully the Browder petition. The failure to get 50 signers in one county would invalidate the petition.

I have already described to you how they scrutinized the petition in the County of Greene.

The Chairman: This requirement of fifty names in the laws of your State, does it apply to all of the counties or to a percentage of counties?

Mr. Browder: All counties. If you fail in one county to get fifty, you are off the ballot. We filed 43,000-and-some signatures. They attacked only in Greene County and, I believe, Franklin County, yes, Greene County and Franklin County were sufficient. The finding in Greene County was that we did not have 50, and so this cancelled all 43,000-some signatures for the whole State.

Further, in the *New York World-Telegram* on September 21, the same political writer on the same subject said:

The polls show that the Labor Party is holding the balance of power now. . . . The fly in the ointment for the Democrats is the threat by the Left-wing leaders that their followers will bolt the Roosevelt-

Wallace ticket.... At any rate the Democrats are determined that if they can prevent Mr. Browder having a place on the ballot they will do so in order to prevent the Left-wing Laborites from having a place to go.... National Chairman Edward J. Flynn is prepared to inspect every signature on the Browder petitions ...

The kind of inspection I have already described.

Further and more directly to this whole question; I quote from the Jewish newspaper, *The Day,* New York, October 11, 1940, with the full translation of the article that I will quote from attached. I want to read just the following quotations in order to be very brief, although the whole article is very interesting and illuminating. Mr. Slonim, the author of that article, wrote:

One feels that if the Roosevelt election campaign will not take on a dynamic character, it can slow up entirely—"and so Roosevelt has taken over the entire leadership into his own hands." New York is absolutely vitally important for Willkie's success. Should he lose New York State, he is lost.

According to all polls taken to date, the situation in New York is not yet certain. Should one and one-half per cent move from one camp to the other, such a shift could give the State to either Willkie or Roosevelt.

"We will win," Ed Flynn told this writer. "We must conduct a campaign as though there were really danger, we must punch and punch and punch again until the day of elections."

Then Mr. Slonim, explaining one of the most important directions for the punches, reported: Under a sub-heading immediately following that quotation, it says: "What will happen to the Communists and Earl Browder?" He then says—the whole article being based upon a press interview between the newspaper writer and Mr. Flynn:

This, too, is an important question in a campaign in New York State. Ed Flynn, himself, who was formerly Secretary of State in New York, is convinced that Browder will not be a candidate [this was after the petitions were filed in Albany]. Mr. Flynn said he was convinced that Browder will not be a candidate. He made no secret of this at a press conference. He said that all signatures on Browder's petitions would be carefully investigated and he therefore would not be a candidate.

The Democrats believe that if Browder is not on the ballot, then all or at least a great number of Communists will be compelled to vote for Roosevelt. How the Communists will vote, I cannot say, but that Browder will not be on the ballot, this I can predict almost with certainty.

Four days after this was printed, the Secretary of State of New York certified the Communist Party to go on the ballot, the time for challenges having elapsed and no challenge having been registered except a challenge which was overruled.

The Chairman: Mr. Browder, referring to the city judge who rendered the decision, Judge Murray, are you able to tell us whether or not Judge Murray is a Republican or Democrat in his political affiliations?

Mr. Browder: From my own knowledge, no, but his general reputation is that he is a Democrat, elected as a Democrat on the Democratic ticket. I know it only by conversations. I have to be very careful in my answers on this.

The Chairman: I want it made clear that by asking that question I am not raising any question as to whether that would influence or not the city judge in the rendering of the decision. It was just in connection with the statement that you had made that there was political significance in an attempt to prevent your name going on the ticket or that of your party, and in connection with that, I thought it was pertinent to inquire.

It is not for the purpose of even suggesting in the remotest way questioning the judge's decision.

Mr. Browder: I understand and I won't make any such question either, and, further, I won't emphasize the political affiliation of any particular person involved in this or other cases that I will cite because it is our experience that whether the motive for an attack comes from the Democratic circles or Republican circles, and in one state it is one case and in another state it is another, that in each case they always get co-operation from at least some individuals in the other party and this is true in New York also.

I won't place it on any narrow partisan basis. There are some people in the Republican Party who are very anxious also to achieve the objectives that the Democrats are working for and vice versa. Formal party lines mean less and less.

Now, I think I have given you a picture of the situation in New York State. It is unquestionably because the Communist Party refused to continue the voluntary support that we gave in the past in New York State to the Democratic candidates who were at the same time common candidates for the American Labor Party that this attack has been made upon us. In depriving us of our ballot rights they hope that they will get, by the force of circumstances, what before they got from us voluntarily.

This is further confirmed by the fact that as late as July of this year, we were approached by persons whom we had every reason to believe did not speak for themselves alone who suggested the advisability of continued collaboration in 1940 as it had been in the past, and when that collaboration was not forthcoming we knew we were in for hard times in New York State as well as all over the country.

Of course, this Committee is not interested in the troubles of the Communist Party, but when these troubles of the Communist Party begin to take the form of a general attack on the sanctity of the electoral processes and establish precedences which, if allowed to stand in relation to Communists, will endanger the rights of all people, will endanger the whole democratic process and which will influence one way or the other the results of a Presidential election and cast a shadow upon such results, then it is time that more attention is given to it than any attention that might be brought merely by sympathy with a persecuted minority....

Abridged stenographic report, Washington, D. C., October 25, 1940.

X. LABOR MUST FIND ITS POLITICAL INDEPENDENCE

JOHN L. LEWIS, in his historic speech of October 25, broke away from the active and official leader of the war party, Roosevelt, only to fall into the arms of the candidate for leadership of that same war party, Willkie. Thus did he give dramatic expression to the most fundamental issue facing labor and the people—the necessity of full political independence from the moribund Democratic and Republican parties which are but two expressions of the war party coalition—without, however, indicating the only radical solution, which is an independent national Labor Party. Labor is still the prisoner of the capitalist two-party system, and Mr. Lewis' most staunch supporters throughout the country will feel a pang of deep disappointment that he passed up his magnificent opportunity to make the first smash through these prison walls, for the sake of the future, but chose rather the short-sighted course, of once again bargaining for crumbs from the table of the rich, of "rewarding friends and punishing enemies," of playing one group of the ruling class against another in competition for labor's support.

When is labor to emerge into its rightful independence, power and dignity, if this poor game is to be forever continued on the plea of the difficulties of independence, and the pauper's profits of the old opportunist game? That is the main question which the progressive labor movement puts before itself and before John L. Lewis. And that is the question to which he contributed no beginnings of an answer.

With Lewis' scorching excoriation of the betrayal of Roosevelt, of his adventurous playing with the welfare, lives, and peace of the people, a profound assent arises from the masses, a deep-voiced "Amen." That is a truth most necessary for the spokesmen of progressive labor and the people to utter loudly and clearly. The myth of the New Deal, now abandoned and betrayed, had to be dispelled. Someone had to stand up and cry out the obvious truth: "The King is naked!" Lewis did it, and thus far performed an historic service.

But the unconditional endorsement of Willkie, as the opposite of Roosevelt, flies in the face of truth and commonsense. It transcends even the moss-grown plausibilities of the "lesser evil" theory. It is incredible. It strikes no answering chord among the masses. It does not correspond to their experience or their understanding. For the masses know that Willkie has pledged himself to follow the selfsame course as Roosevelt in every essential, to do the very things for which Roosevelt is so justly and roundly repudiated. The act does not ring true. It is the expedient of the moment, the grasping of a straw. It is an expression of weakness, not of strength, a weakness which, if not remedied, can become fatal in the unfolding of events as history whirls forward.

There can be nothing but contempt for the howls and caviling against Lewis, which come from the camp of Roosevelt's "labor" lieutenants. Among these Lilliputians, Lewis has stood forth as a giant. They have groveled at the feet of the war machine and would deliver labor in chains for the reward of Roosevelt's smile. Lewis has at least tried to bargain for some definite gain as the price of labor's vote, even though such bargain is dubious and unsound, and dangerous for the future.

The Communists have no part or parcel with endorsement of Willkie, unconditional or otherwise. Once entrenched in power, he will ruthlessly drive forward the program of imperialist reaction and war which Roosevelt ruthlessly drives forward today. That is why the Communist Party and its growing mass of supporters fight so fiercely for the people's ballot rights in New York today. For the Communist Party in 1940 occupies the unique position of being the only channel through which labor and the masses can register unequivocally their will to peace, their struggle for a better life, their path to the future when labor will hold all power in its own hands.

Sunday Worker, *October 27, 1940.*

XI. SHALL IT BE WAR?

MR. DREISER has eloquently expressed what millions of Americans are thinking tonight.* These are the thoughts which unite the Communist Party at this moment with these millions. The all-important question before our country is this: Shall America be plunged into the catastrophe of the imperialist war?

Candidate Willkie has charged that Roosevelt is leading us into the war. That is true, terribly true. The great majority of Americans want to stop this course. But it is also true that each and every step Roosevelt has taken in this direction has received the blessings of Willkie. Are the American people such political children that we shall believe that the selfsame policy with Roosevelt leads to war while with Willkie it will maintain peace? But war is the result of policy, not of mistakes of individuals. And it is policy that is dragging our country swiftly into this war.

The two leading candidates have made it impossible to choose between war and peace by choosing between them. Roosevelt has proved in action that he is rushing America into war. He is restrained for the moment by the imminent election, in which the voters would strongly resent any war moves at this moment. Indeed, we may expect some spectacular "peace gestures" this week, for the one purpose of pacifying a suspicious people. But his course is fixed, and Roosevelt will go "full speed ahead" once he has his mandate.

But Willkie has pledged himself to follow the same path. Once entrenched in power, Willkie will drive ruthlessly forward the

* Earl Browder was introduced to the radio audience by Theodore Dreiser who spoke from California.—*Ed.*

program of imperialist reaction and war which Roosevelt drives forward ruthlessly now. There is but this small difference between them: Roosevelt is already in the driver's seat all set to go, while Willkie wants to occupy that same seat. To choose Willkie might mean, at most, to gain that time occupied in changing drivers, a few weeks or months at best. Truly a miserable choice for the sovereign American voters!

The radical remedy needed for this situation is a Labor Party. This is now too late for the November 5 balloting, but it is not too early to speak for it for future elections, assuming that all elections will not be abolished once the country gives a "mandate" for war. For this election only the Communist Party offers a channel for the Labor Party vote, for a clear alternative policy of a reasonable, realistic, rounded-out peace policy for America.

That is why Democrats and Republicans joined in violently and illegally driving the Communist Party off the ballot in twenty-four states. They want to leave the protest vote no place to go, no way to vote except for war. In Ohio and Illinois especially, where our Party is strong, they took our ticket off the ballot by force and fraud, in fear of the great anti-war vote which it would certainly have registered.

In New York, we have the shameful spectacle of Boss Flynn, campaign manager for Mr. Roosevelt, openly boasting that the Communist Party would be kept off the ballot, to force its vote to go to Roosevelt, and then the courts obediently carried out his instructions; this is done in the face of a fourfold compliance with legal requirements of petition signatures, and in face of the fact that the Communist Party only lost its permanent place on the ballot because in 1938 it withdrew its candidate for Governor in favor of the Democrats, barely saving the state thereby from going Republican and electing Thomas E. Dewey. They pay us for that help by driving us off the ballot altogether. A terrible and sinister blow against free elections, when minority parties, any party, is wiped off the ballot by high-handed administrative edict, by deprivation from jobs, relief, and old-age pensions, by threats of concentration camps, by trumped-up prosecutions and imprisonments, like the sending of the West Virginia farmer, Oscar Wheeler, to prison for fifteen years for gathering signatures to the Communist petitions. Every country that has lost its liberties in these past years has started on the downward path by such suppressions of the Communist Party. What happens to us today will happen to all other oppositions to-morrow.

To voters in those states where the Communist national ticket has been taken from the ballot, I cannot offer any alternative among the other minority parties. In such states we can make no recommendations for President, but only urge the highest possible vote for Congressional and local peace candidates. Norman Thomas is a futile and dangerous muddlehead, whose chief objection to the war is that he wants it to be directed also against the Soviet Union. Other minority parties make no pretense of answering the problems of the day.

In this dilemma of political disfranchisement, each individual voter is thrown back upon his own conscience, to choose between the primitive expedients of (a) the excessively difficult "write in" vote; or (b) abstentionism which violates his instincts to action; or (c) the choice between two evils both of which every fiber of one's being calls to repudiate.

It is a hard choice, where the Communist Party is not on the ballot. All the more reason, therefore, where it is possible to do so, to roll up the biggest possible vote for peace, for security, for free elections, for civil rights, for jobs—by casting your vote for the candidates of the Communist Party.

Speech delivered over the network of the Mutual Broadcasting Company, October 29, 1940.

emphasize the absence of any principle difference between them. Both sides appeal to the electorate with extreme demagogy.

Willkie has bid for the anti-war vote, in order to split Roosevelt's following: Roosevelt has emerged as chief red-baiter, trying to split Willkie's upper-class following with the slogans of anti-Communism. These are the new features of the last ten days of the campaign, together with the trimmings of eggs, onions, knees, and hooliganism generally, with workers being sent to prison for sentences up to fifteen years for daring to attempt to engage in the sacred game of politics without a license from either Roosevelt or Willkie!

We warn the workers and farmers of America that neither of the major parties, nor their candidates, are worthy of the slightest confidence. Both are pledged to spend the life-blood of American youth and the sweat of American labor for the aggrandizement of Wall Street's profits and imperial world power. The turning of old rascals out will only put new rascals in. Whichever one holds power will be the immediate enemy which labor must fight and overcome, if labor would defend its rights, its living standards, and its peace. That is the dilemma posed by the two major parties.

On Friday night Roosevelt disclosed that which he had long kept a secret, namely, that he reads the *Daily Worker*. That is, of course, nothing to hide; all really well-informed people read the *Daily Worker*. But what is interesting is that Roosevelt found there the evidence of something very terrible, a political advertisement paid for by supporters of the Republicans. "Something evil is happening in this country," he said, when such a thing could take place.

Now this is a very interesting problem, indeed, which the President has raised. We are justified in examining it in some detail, because it registers the fact that Communism is now an issue of the day for America.

As to whether the *Daily Worker* should accept political advertising at all, this is a question to be settled among supporters and readers of that paper and its management. There are two opinions on that, but since the paper is no longer the official organ of the Communist Party, it was clearly within the province of the management to accept advertising if it saw fit. Just as newspapers supporting Roosevelt accepted and printed the advertisement, so the *Daily Worker* supporting Browder and Ford printed it, as a matter of business policy, not of politics. But of all papers, only the *Daily Worker* printed a refutation of its arguments in an equally prominent position. So, if Mr. Roosevelt was worried about preserving the purity of Communist principles, we can set his mind at rest.

Of course, Roosevelt had something quite different in mind. He is angry because Boss Flynn blundered in trying to steal the Communist votes for him. He was trying to set up a new rule in American politics, namely, that anyone even remotely associating with the Communists in any way, even to advertising in their papers, shall be registered as suspect and deprived of public office. And then he demanded the application of this rule to his rival, Willkie. This is a strange proposal from the Democrats who, in the State of New York, hold power as against the Republicans, only by the margin of votes gives them by the Communist Party in 1938. And it was the Communist Party which terminated that association—Democrats were still vainly soliciting our support in New York as late as July, 1940, with the knowledge of Roosevelt. Since they couldn't reach the grapes for themselves, they now warn the Republicans that the grapes are sour.

On the question of the Communist votes, let me console both Democrats and Republicans. We are not going to allow our votes to strengthen either of you. We will use our votes to undermine and defeat both of you, your war plans together with your whole system of private ownership of the country by a handful of monopolists. And we will know how to accomplish this even though you have illegally and arbitrarily removed our ticket from the ballot in New York, in Ohio, in Illinois, and in twenty-one other states, even though you have railroaded forty-three of our best workers to prison in Pennsylvania for daring to put our Party on the ballot, even though you sent Oscar Wheeler to prison in West Virginia for fifteen years for soliciting signatures to our petitions!

For you can neither intimidate nor corrupt the Communist Party. This is the reason why Democratic and Republican politicians fear the Communist Party. And that is why growing hundreds of thousands of working people respect and love our Party.

The immediate perspective for American working people is a dark one. Regardless of who wins the elections, war and reaction will ride the seats of power, and only the most fearless and resolute struggle can put any check upon them. For this struggle we must prepare; for this struggle we must gather and register strength in the voting on November 5.

Hard struggles, ever more severe trials, lie ahead for the working class and for the Communist Party. There is no place today for a facile and shallow optimism, which promises easy victories, at little cost. There is nothing of the sort in prospect.

Yet we face the future with serene confidence. In the broadest and deepest sense we are enthusiastically optimistic. And this optimism is based not upon faith alone, but upon concrete facts and experiences.

In this election campaign, we have seen the struggle for political independence of the working class go ahead a big step in the beginnings of the mass breakaway from the Roosevelt illusion; a Willkie can never rebuild for 1944 the old obstacle that prevented the Labor Party from appearing in 1940.

In this election campaign the masses of the labor and peace movements, even though faced with the Willkie-Roosevelt agreement on policy against them, have made their influence felt, have registered their will to peace, have prepared a storm for any government which overrides that will and takes America into the imperialist war.

These are the signs of approaching maturity of the American working class, which alone can build a new America as part of a new world, a world of socialism.

Roosevelt and Willkie join in denouncing the Communists as "foreign agents," as "representatives of an alien way of life," as "agents of Stalin." It is significant that they find Norman Thomas and the Socialist Party no danger to the capitalist "way of life."

Soviet Union's Example

No, we Communists are not agents of Stalin. We are, however, emulators of Stalin. The achievements which Stalin has led in gaining for the Soviet Union, we would strive to gain for the United States and its people.

The Soviet Union has maintained peace with its neighbors, has kept neutral toward the imperialist war, has defeated all attempts to draw it in—to the great benefit of its people. America, on the contrary, has abandoned neutrality, has become deeply involved, and is in imminent danger of becoming a belligerent. The Communist Party would save America from catastrophe by emulating the policy of Stalin.

The Soviet Union has multiplied its industrial production tenfold since 1929, made its defenses impregnable, and at the same time raised the general standard of living by 500 per cent. The Communist Party would do the same for the United States, emulating the policy of Stalin, which achieved these history-making figures.

We Communists have the deepest confidence in the American people. We say that Americans can accomplish anything that other peoples can. If the Russians can increase their national income by one thousand per cent during eleven or twelve years, we say that Americans could do the same thing once we adopted the corresponding policies and leadership. If the Russians can maintain peace and security, in a warlike world, so could we Americans.

But that would require that we understand the cause and origin of our present troubles and disasters, and remove it. That cause and origin is the decaying and broken-down system of capitalism, which Mr. Roosevelt describes as a system of "private profit and private enterprise," which for Mr. Willkie is "the American way of life." That is the system of monopoly, in which a small fraction of the population owns most of the national economy, in which the masses must find work as wage-labor, a system which is the negation of democracy, which can no longer feed the people, which inevitably breeds crises and wars.

Twenty-three years ago next Thursday, the workers and farmers of the former tsarist empire under the leadership of Lenin overthrew the power of their capitalists and landlords, established a new regime of their own, which they called Soviets, or Councils, and began to build the new system of socialism out of the ruins of the old society destroyed by the war. That was the beginning and the foundation of the tremendous advances and achievements of the Soviet Union today under the leadership of Stalin.

America has much to teach the Soviet Union in the way of technique, but the Soviet Union has more to teach us, in the matter of finding the social and economic forms which will put technique and science in the service of all the people.

No people is free or can maintain peace unless it owns and controls its own economy, the material foundation of society. If that economy is in the hands of a privileged class, the people are not free, there can be no democracy, there can be no peace.

The only way the masses of the people can own and control a modern economy of power-machine production is through collective ownership and operation, that is, through socialism.

The Soviet Union is showing us the first practical working out of socialism. Its achievements are the proof of the superiority of socialism over capitalism.

Therefore we must learn from the experience of the Soviet Union if we wish America to go forward, to increase its wealth and the well being of its people, to maintain peace.

Only the working class, when it has gained its independence from the capitalists and their agents, from the bourgeoisie, can bring socialism into existence, can build a new world.

This is the message of the Communist Party of the United States to the American people.

This is why the Democratic and Republican parties, Roosevelt and Willkie, unite in persecuting the Communist Party and denouncing communism before the country, because both of them represent the monopolists who hold the private ownership of American economy, who make private profits from it, and who rule the American people by this means, and who are driving us into imperialist war.

This is why the capitalists, the bourgeoisie, fear and hate the Communist Party, because they know they can never meet its challenge, because they know their old system is dying, because they know the Communist Party represents the inevitable future.

This is why the Communist Party can never be suppressed, can never be defeated, can never be destroyed, no matter how fiercely or ruthlessly the present ruling powers may attack it.

This is why the Democrats and Republicans, the more desperately they fight against us, only the more surely and effectively educate the masses in the truth of our program.

This is why we can say that no matter how the ballots are cast on November 5, only the Communist Party has strengthened its hold among the people, has deepened their confidence, has prepared them for the solution of their problems.

This is why we can claim that it is the Communist Party that is emerging as the victor, that all other parties are registering their decay, the preparations for their demise.

For the road to life, to prosperity, to peace, to the future, is the road to socialism. And this road is charted only by the Communist Party.

Speech delivered at Madison Square Garden, November 3, 1940.

XIII. RESULTS OF THE 1940 ELECTIONS

On November 6, the cry went up from leading circles of both Republican and Democratic parties that now, since the elections are over, all campaign documents and speeches should be immediately and publicly burned, with appropriate ceremonials, and should be forgotten as quickly as possible. Norman Thomas even rushed the gun, and sent this message over the air before midnight of November 5, immediately following Boss Flynn's announcement of victory for the third term.

This common thought of all the "great minds" arises from their common recognition that, despite all the best laid plans, the election campaign did get out of hand, it took a course in its last days quite displeasing to them all, and they all found themselves saying things they want forgotten immediately and completely. Elemental forces had broken through the most complete blockade, finding powerful, if distorted, expression. And the gentlemen at the top are uneasy about it, they are disturbed, they want it wiped from the popular mind.

What a revealing commentary this is upon the true character of our boasted democracy! Almost before the election is over, its leading participants and their servants hasten to tell the masses that the decisive period of the political debate, the ten days before the voting, consisted of lies, slanders, appeals to prejudice, unsound arguments, of which we must all be ashamed and forget as quickly as possible!

The Communist Party has no need to wash itself after the election in this manner. We have nothing in our campaign of which we are ashamed, nothing we wish forgotten, no speeches or documents which we are not ready to defend after the election with equal or greater conviction. Instead of burning our campaign speeches, we sent to press the day after election a permanent pamphlet of the Presidential campaign addresses, copies of which are in your hands, which we believe you will unanimously endorse.

One outstanding feature of the election campaign in its last phase was described by Karl Marx over ninety years ago, in words which for concise and appropriate description of America in 1940 cannot be improved upon. In the introduction to *The Communist Manifesto,* Marx said:

Where is the party in opposition that has not been decried as communistic by its opponents in power? Where the Opposition that has not hurled back the branding reproach of Communism, against the more advanced opposition parties, as well as against its reactionary adversaries?

Wendell Willkie was doubtless unconscious of the fact that he was following the Marxian law to the letter when he accused Roosevelt of communistic tendencies. Roosevelt was equally unconscious of how he was proving the genius of Marx when he accused Willkie of seeking an alliance with the Communists. Their ignorance of fundamental political laws, however, only emphasizes the profound correctness of Marx's conclusion from similar phenomena almost a century ago, namely, that *"Communism is already acknowledged by all ... to be itself a power."* True in 1848, and a thousand times true in 1940!

How the Masses Intervened in This Election

Even before the major party conventions, it was already clear and registered by us that, whatever the election outcome, the chief executive office would be occupied by the War Party coalition, by a representative of Wall Street. After the nominations this fact was publicly confirmed when Willkie at Elwood quoted the exact words of Roosevelt as their common war platform, and repeated his promises on domestic policy. In the first phase of the campaign, up to October 2, this agreement was rigidly adhered to. Under its cover were put over the two great decisive steps toward militarization and war, the conscription law and the alliance with the British Empire. But already the pact between the war coalition was strained, because the election campaign was on, and the masses were pressing upon both parties and their leaders their profound abhorrence of the war.

The first decisive break in the war coalition of the bourgeoisie— they call it "national unity"—came on the conscription issue, when in Congress two-thirds of Republican Representatives and one-third of the whole House, including Democrats, voted against the draft bill, defying their official leaders and the enormous pressure from above, in concession to the rising pressure of the masses from below. The trade of fifty destroyers for naval bases with Britain and the Joint Defense Council with belligerent Canada were not even submitted to Congress as accomplished facts, but were carried through as edicts of a military dictatorship. This was unquestionably due to fear of crystallization of a strong opposition in the country, and not to the inherent dictatorial tendencies of Roosevelt, for it weakened rather than strengthened his immediate position, whatever its significance as a precedent for the future, since it registered a fear of the people and even of Congress. The masses had begun to register their profound opposition to the war, despite and over the head of the rigged-up election combination.

From this moment the course of the election campaign changed its character. What had been planned by the coalition as a great drive to whip up war hysteria among the masses, leading to a war mandate on November 5, broke down and took another course. Willkie awoke to the fact that his candidacy was fading into nothingness. In his Cleveland speech he suddenly switched tactics (without in any way modifying his programmatic commitments) and made a definite appeal for the anti-war vote, accusing Roosevelt of planning to take the country into the war, which he pledged his election would prevent. The rise in his political prospects was sudden and dramatic, although that speech cost him the support of some of his original backers, and Dorothy Thompson—an army in her own right—deserted him for the President. So menacing became the peace issue to the third-term prospect that Roosevelt was finally forced to revise his plans and enter the campaign speaking lists. Instead of being able to whip up the war spirit further, Roosevelt was forced to engage in competition with Willkie in promises of peace.

Thus, instead of the election result being, as planned, a mandate for the war policy, it was turned into its opposite, a registration of the fact that no candidate could win the country on a war platform so long as there was even the most shallow and demagogic appeal to the masses for peace by the other chief candidate. That the promises of both candidates were sheer demagogy, there is hardly need for me to emphasize here. The peace promises were concessions to mass sentiment, wrung from two unwilling candidates. They were maneuvers to deceive and cheat the masses—but they have a value, if the masses, especially the workers, strengthen their independent organizations with the determination to enforce these promises in a serious strugggle against the war-makers. The turn of the campaign, in which the masses compelled the recognition of their desire for peace, as shown in the change from demagogy for war to demagogy about peace, was a great victory for the workers, for the people. It was the outstanding feature, the surprise, of a campaign which in its beginning appeared on the surface to be cut-and-dried.

The Disintegration of Old Party Ties

Superficial and tendencious commentators are already busy interpreting the distribution of votes on November 5, as an unprecedented strengthening of the hold of the Democratic and Republican parties upon the masses. The true significance of this election is quite to the contrary.

The superficial argument runs, that with the biggest poll in American history, close to fifty millions, the vote cast for all the minor parties taken as a whole was the smallest in modern times. A larger percentage of votes went for the two major parties than has occurred at any time in the twentieth century—this in the face of the closest programmatic agreement between the major parties that has ever appeared during this time.

It would be the greatest mistake to accept this surface appearance at its face value. Allegiance to the two old parties among the masses has never been so weak as it is now. It is notorious that the Democratic Party has long been held together only by the mass prestige of the New Deal Roosevelt who was opposed by the majority of his own party leaders. Roosevelt's abandonment of the New Deal for an armaments, militarization and war policy has so profoundly alienated the masses who followed him with enthusiasm in 1936 that in 1940 they voted for him with obvious reluctance, with suspicion, and only because Willkie was committed to identical policies and was obviously dishonest in his last-minute peace demagogy. There is not the slightest doubt that a Republican candidate who would have opposed conscription, the hysterical military appropriations and the deal with Britain—even such an old-fashioned conservative as Taft—would have won handily in most states outside the Solid South. The hold of the Democratic Party, and of Roosevelt, upon the masses has been seriously shaken and undermined, far beyond the measure of the drop from 62 per cent of the vote in 1936 to 55 per cent in 1940.

As for the Republican Party, its morale, which reflects its ties with the masses, was so low that its convention in Philadelphia could be stampeded into abandoning all its known and traditional leaders in favor of an unknown, a Democrat in all his previous political activity, and who was chosen precisely because he was politically a blank sheet of paper upon which each voter could be invited to write his own prescription and vote for it. Surely, that is no evidence of a hold upon the masses. Even Willkie's increase of votes over Landon was won only in the last weeks, after he departed from his coalition program to engage in desperate demagogy.

A further evidence of the weakening of the ties of both parties with the masses is the unprecedented shifting from one side to the other. The appearance of this phenomenon among well-known public figures only reflected a much more significant shifting among the masses of the voters. More than in any modern campaign, the theory of the "lesser evil" came forward as a major manifestation. The votes were more "against" than "for."

The Socialist Party vote for Norman Thomas is not yet known fully or exactly. But from fragmentary returns, it is already clear that it shows a rather complete collapse and bankruptcy. In New York City it ran below the exceedingly difficult "write-in" vote for the Communist Party. The ambiguous, banal, weasel-worded, toadying campaign of Norman Thomas met its natural and inevitable response among the voters, even those who for years had followed him and his party banner faithfully. It had finally become more than they could stomach.

The Communist Party, denied a place on the ballot in more than half the states, including centers of our greatest strength such as New York, Ohio, and Illinois, had not even the physical possibility of measuring its mass influence by the vote cast for its candidates. Considering the unprecedented campaign, official and unofficial, of intimidation and suppression carried on against our Party, it can only be judged as a many-times multiplied mass influence as compared with 1936, to have reached or even surpassed that vote in 1940.

It has always been difficult to get Communist votes cast, and even more difficult to get them counted. In order to get some measure of how much mass influence our Party must have in order to register a hundred thousand votes in the Presidential election, let us resort to a bit of imaginative comparison. Let us suppose, for example, that Mr. Willkie and his party, even with all their financial and propertied backing, had nevertheless been forced to enter this campaign with a law on Federal statute books denying public employment or relief to any Republican; with the courts revoking naturalization papers of any citizen shown to have been a Republican when naturalized; with a Congressional Committee holding public inquisitions to ferret out hidden Republicans to drive them out of public or private employment, and to instigate any and every possible legal proceedings against them; with their party forced to gather signatures to petitions to get on the ballot, with public blacklisting in the newspapers of such signers; with their election workers imprisoned by the hundreds and assaulted by the thousands, with a Republican candidate for governor in one state sentenced to prison for fifteen years for the obvious fraud of obtaining signatures to its petitions on the ground that the Republican Party is "the Party of Lincoln"; with the party finally thrown off the ballot in most of the states; with no prospects of gain for anyone but only of sacrifice; with a thousand and one other large and petty persecutions. With all this, one can only speculate how many votes Mr. Wendell Willkie or Mr. Roosevelt will be able to register, if and when they are brought by fate to face similar conditions. For such conditions are a real test of how deep a party's roots have penetrated among the masses.

The Re-Emergence of the Labor Party Movement

A major and most important feature of the election campaign was registered during its last ten days in the sudden and emphatic re-emergence of the Labor Party movement. This occurred in the very heat of the final campaign drive, when the Labor Party could not even dream of finding organizational expression, when the masses were already making up their minds which of the two evils should be chosen as the lesser one. Following the historic radio broadcast of John L. Lewis on October 25, which placed this dilemma in its sharpest form, a large part of the most representative progressive trade unions and people's organizations, with their leaders, responded with an unequivocal declaration of lack of confidence in both major candidates, with the demand for labor's political independence in the form of a Labor Party, together with unswerving adherence to the firmly established progressive policies of the C.I.O., as led by John L. Lewis.

There is no need here to repeat the timely and correct evaluation of this event which our Party made at the time. What we need to record and emphasize now is the tremendous historical significance of this upsurge of the demand for labor's complete political independence, at the very climax of a hotly contested election, from which labor had been excluded except as voting-cattle. The great significance of this event is in nowise diminished by the fact that, as individuals, the members and leaders of these organizations in most cases chose a "lesser evil" on November 5, and divided their ballots between Roosevelt and Willkie; neither is it diminished by any momentary confusions that may have appeared in progressive ranks during those days. On the whole, it must be said that the progressive circles, rank and file and leaders, displayed a brilliant capacity to seize the moment for a smashing blow against the camp of the warmongers, together with their agents in the labor movement, and for upholding the arms of all fighters for peace and progress.

A tremendous latent "third party" or Labor Party movement was present in the 1940 campaign, hidden by the surface of events, but revealing itself, beyond any doubt, to close observation and analysis. It could not come forward for lack of timely and bold leadership. But this is a lack which can be remedied, as was shown so forcibly by the re-emergence of the demand for a Labor Party in the last days of the campaign.

This great Labor Party manifestation was another sign of the distintegration of the old bourgeois parties, of their loosening hold upon the masses, of the imminent emergence of a new party on the American political scene, through which labor will achieve its independence and rally to its side the farmers and all toiling masses, in a great mass struggle for political power.

How the Communist Party Worked in the Campaign

We have already given a general and rough estimate of the Communist vote and its significance, as showing multiplied influence and deepening roots among the masses. It is now necessary to examine how our Party worked in this campaign to bring about such a result.

First of all, we multiplied our strength because under the most extreme difficulties we never allowed ourselves to be cut off from that source of all strength, the masses of workers, of the people. We never allowed ourselves to drift or be driven into sectarianism. We went to the masses, we had faith in the masses, we drew strength from the masses, we gave leadership to the masses. This campaign was for us, from first to last, a mass campaign.

We have already described that great victory of the masses, their intervention in the election campaign, how they frustrated the original plans of the two-party coalition to make it a war campaign, how they forced the change from a demagogy for war to a demagogy about peace. That mass intervention was a spontaneous, unorganized movement on the whole. But its success was determined by the presence within it of elements of organization and leadership. Without some elements of clarity, organization and leadership no success is possible, and the degree of success of a mass movement is always commensurate with the degree to which these factors are present.

These important and vital factors of clarity, organization and leadership were furnished, in the first place, by the Communist Party. Alone among all nationally-organized political forces, the Communist Party foresaw the possibility of this intervention of the masses, and worked consciously, systematically and energetically to bring it into motion and direct it to success. *Not* the Communist Party *alone,* of course, but the Party attracting and guiding and working through the broadest circles of militant progressives, did this work. But the Communist Party *alone* was a nationally-organized directing center conscious of its goal. Thereby we won thousands of devoted adherents and new friends.

So, also, in the loosening of the ties between the old parties and the masses, the process comes spontaneously out of the relations of class forces and their struggles, but it is given consciousness, direction and effectiveness by the work of our Party, in the first instance. When the party in power decries its opposition as communistic, when the opposition hurls back that reproach, not only against the more advanced opposition parties but also against its chief adversary, as we witnessed so sharply in this campaign in the United States, we have learned from Marx to recognize this as the consequence of the emergence of Communism as a power, acknowledged as such by all. Our Communist Party by its work forced the two major parties, which held 99 per cent of the vote, nevertheless to recognize and combat Communism as their most significant and dangerous opposition, and to recriminate each other as to supposed Communistic tendencies within themselves.

So, also, in the upsurge of the Labor Party movement, the bourgeoisie and its ideologists can see nothing but the manifestation of Communism. Of course the Communist Party supported this movement, and furnished its most conscious element. But it is a broad mass movement, going far beyond our Party ranks. When the capitalist press brands this movement and its leaders as "Communist," it is only repeating the same formula under which Willkie and Roosevelt hurled this epithet at one another.

The Communist Party gave support to every clearly progressive and peace candidate even if he ran on the Democratic or Republican ticket. All the more so did we support that wing of the American Labor Party in New York which revolted against the old warmongering, reactionary, and Social-Democratic state leadership. Here again, of course, the war camp instantly and unanimously brands any and every opposition to its course as "Communist" beyond the slightest shadow of doubt! The grain of truth behind this lie is that the Communists support everything seriously progressive, and that without the existence of the Communist Party all progressives would find this world a darker and more difficult place.

The Rose-Antonini-Dubinsky-Hillman warmongering leadership within the American Labor Party are boasting of their great election victories. "They" carried the state for Roosevelt. Let them take responsibility, therefore, for what Roosevelt gives to labor, beginning with the $112,000,000 war contract to Henry Ford in the days immediately following election. But it was the progressive wing of the American Labor Party, against the most bitter and energetic opposition of the pro-war leaders, which gave the A.L.P. its only independent electoral victories, outstandingly the sweeping victory of Vito Marcantonio, the fighting Congressman from Harlem. Marcantonio was plastered on every billboard and in every newspaper as a "Communist," because of his brilliant fight against militarization and his generally progressive record, but his constituents, by no means Communists, and largely Catholics, returned him to Congress over his Tammany opponent by a majority of almost two to one. That was a great tribute to Marcantonio; it was also a demonstration that the masses do not agree that it is so terrible to come under the accusation of being a Communist.

Out of the whole campaign, and out of the work of the Communist Party in it, it is clear that we have emerged far stronger than we have been before. And I repeat, this is above all because we took our correct understanding and policy to the masses, and always to the masses.

THE HIGH IMPORTANCE OF THE FIGHT FOR THE BALLOT

The Communist Party's election campaign was, from beginning to end, a prolonged and bitter fight to establish our place on the ballot in the various states. Our Party's members and supporters conducted the struggle with heroism and devotion, enlisting several hundred thousand persons directly in one or another form in this fundamental battle to resist the deterioration and destruction of the democratic achievements of the American people. Our casualties ranged all the way from thousands blacklisted from their jobs, hundreds beaten up, multilated and jailed, scores sentenced to prison terms on frame-up charges, and one, Oscar Wheeler, candidate for Governor in West Virginia, sentenced to fifteen years' imprisonment for soliciting signatures on the ground that his arguments for support to the Communist candidates were "fraudulent." But throughout the fight, our Party did not weaken or capitulate for a single moment; it carried the battle through right up to the end.

It is not my purpose to review all the rich detail of this struggle at this time, valuable as such an examination would be, nor to search out the many shortcomings and weaknesses which inevitably accompanied this so generally admirable and well-conducted campaign. Others will contribute to this task of review and analysis.

At this point what is most necessary is to fix the main historical significance and political lessons of the battle for the ballot.

Two points stand out in any such political estimate: First, the Communist Party's fight for its ballot rights was the front line of struggle for all the immediate demands of the working class and the majority of the people. Every nation that has lost its liberties and been thrown into catastrophe in these last years started on the downward path by the suppression of the Communist Party. By fighting for the legality and full election rights of the Communist Party, we were fighting for no narrow party interest, but for peace, for democratic rights and civil liberties, for protection of the standards of life, for the whole working class and the nation.

Second, this fight for the ballot was a fundamental step in the political education of the American masses, necessary for their understanding of the class nature of bourgeois democracy, of the dictatorship of monopoly capital that is exercised through democratic forms, of the inevitable course taken by monopoly capital toward the destruction of these democratic forms whenever they begin to limit and hamper the supremacy of Wall Street's rule. It was necessary to demonstrate to the masses, through their own experience, that it is a lie that the Communists are the enemies of democracy, that in truth it is always the most vicious anti-Communists who first and most destructively tear down and destroy even the limited democratic rights previously enjoyed by the masses. The fight for the ballot was a primer of political education, a concrete American version in terms of experience, of Lenin's immortal book, *State and Revolution*.

PERSPECTIVES AND TASKS

This report is not intended as a complete and rounded-out review of the elections, their issues, the experiences, and all the detailed lessons. Much of what is to be said has already been dealt with in editorials and articles in the *Daily Worker*, with more to follow, and these things are repeated and developed in this report only in so far as necessary to fix the main, the outstanding, the decisive characteristics.

A few words are required as to the perspectives. While no one can predict the exact form in which the imperialist war will develop, and in which America will be fully involved, yet one thing is clear: The ruling classes of the United States are riding ruthlessly into the middle of the bloody imperialist war for the redivision of the world; fear of revolutionary unheaval in Europe, and the determination to hold it down by all means, remains the most powerful general motive driving American ruling circles toward entrance into the war as a belligerent. This is already tied up most closely with the Far East which, through the Dutch East Indies (Indonesia), may well be the door for United States' entrance into the second World War. Capitalism must be preserved at all costs abroad if Wall Street is to feel safe in America; that is the meaning behind all the hypocritical battle cries under which American youth is being mobilized as cannon fodder.

For the working classes and toiling masses, therefore, the future is one of intensifying struggle to keep out of the war, and to bring the war to an end; of ever broader and more serious battles to defeat and throw back the attacks of monopoly capital against wages and living standards, against social legislation, against civil liberties and democratic rights for the masses. This struggle will inevitably force a general recognition among the working class and the toiling masses that the two old parties represent their enemy, Wall Street, monopoly capital, the economic royalists; that it is necessary to break completely with these parties, and achieve political independence through a Labor Party or Farmer-Labor Party.

The trade unions are again coming forth as the most important and decisive factor in this struggle, in all its phases. Now more than ever before the trade unions must be extended and consolidated; must perfect their own inner democracy, so that the will of the broad rank and file will be truly reflected in a progressive, clear-headed and militant leadership; must rally around themselves the farmers, the Negroes, the youth, all the democratic organizations and masses of the country.

In the welter of imperialist war plans, formed and being carried out by the most reactionary and undemocratic forces of American life, it has become a matter of life and death for the democratic forces of America—indispensably led by labor—to intervene in the whole sphere of the foreign policy of this country. As, at the dawn of our nationhood, a rejection of the fatal foreign policy engendered within the sordid reactionary forces of American political life, and the acceptance of Jefferson's proposed foreign policy of peace based upon the strength of co-operation with the revolutionary republican forces of Europe, brought this the young American Republic to safety— just so, today, the American working class heirs of the revolutionary republican Jefferson must work for the safety of their democratic heritage by compelling a foreign policy of co-operation with the only remaining powerful progressive forces of Europe, with the Union of Soviet Socialist Republics. Those who in America strive to alienate the United States from, and to continue the present foreign policy of tricky hypocrisy and sabotage of relations with, the Union of Soviet Socialist Republics, are playing the same treacherous role toward America as was played by the Petains and Weygands, the Lavals, Daladiers and Blums in breaking up the keystone of France's security—her mutual aid pact with the strongest power of Europe, the Union of Soviet Socialist Republics. The imperative duty of the American workers and all their democratic allies is to fight for the strength and peace of America through the most cordial relations and co-operation with the Soviet Union and with the struggling democracy of China.

American workers must be brought ever closer in information, understanding and common action with the workers and democratic mass movements of the Latin American countries. They must be rallied to the most immediate concrete aid to the rescue of the Spanish republican refugees in France, and their transportation and resettlement in Latin America, supporting the campaign already launched by the United Spanish Aid Committee; and learn how to help the Spanish people prepare to overthrow the Franco fascist dictatorship. They must be rallied to more energetic aid to the heroic Chinese people, fighting for their national independence against United States' munitions furnished to the Japanese imperialists. They must learn to understand and help the workers of the European lands who, on both sides of the battlelines, are preparing their forces for the overthrow of their capitalist, imperialist, fascist oppressors and destroyers.

These are the perspectives and tasks of labor and the toiling masses. The perspectives and tasks of the Communist Party can only be the same, with the Communist Party in the forefront as the most far-sighted, the most advanced, the most organized, the most persistent, the most courageous, the most reliable detachment of the working class.

To play such a role, the Communist Party must give the most serious attention to building its own forces, to recruiting new members, to educating itself and its supporters ever more thoroughly, to mastering the theory and practice of scientific socialism, which is communism. These are our perspectives and tasks. Let us move forward with deeper confidence and determination, knowing that we represent the masses and the future.

Report to the National Committee of the Communist Party, New York, November 16, 1940.

PART THREE

THE WAY OUT OF THE IMPERIALIST WAR

I. PROLETARIAN INTERNATIONALISM

It was Abraham Lincoln, representative of the best American tradition, who expressed a fundamental principle of social progress when he uttered these immortal words:

The strongest bond of human sympathy, outside of the family relationship, should be one uniting all working people, of all nations and tongues and kindreds.

In these words, uttered in 1864 in accepting honorary membership in the Workingmen's Association of New York, Lincoln adopted as his own the same fundamental thought which Marx and Engels had embodied in the historic *Communist Manifesto* of 1848, with its concluding slogan: "Workingmen of all countries, unite!"

The principle of international solidarity that was brought into world history by the modern labor movement and incorporated in the First International is not only not in conflict with the traditions of this country, but is an inseparable part of the most heroic chapter of American history. The International Workingmen's Association (the First International) was founded in the very struggle of the European working classes, and came into existence on the impetus of their struggle to prevent the destruction of the United States of America by European intervention in 1863-64 in the American Civil War on behalf of the slave power. It was the profound understanding of Lincoln of the inseparable connection of the modern labor movement with the life and development of the democratic current of history that enabled the greatest of American Presidents to welcome the proffered aid of the First International and its Communist founders, Marx and Engels, whose inspiration and active organizational work brought about the great mass movement of British labor that prevented the intervention by the British navy that had been planned by Lord Palmerston and approved by the British cabinet and monarch. There is no conflict between the international solidarity of labor and the interests of the American nation; and those who try—though in vain—to eliminate the ineradicable internationalism of American labor are reactionary enemies, not only of labor, but of democracy and of the American nation itself.

Since Lincoln's time, this fundamental idea has gained almost universal acceptance. Today, in America, even the reactionary leadership of the American Federation of Labor must at least pay lip service to this principle, in its paper project of a Pan-American Federation of Labor under its direction, and in its formal affiliation to the International Federation of Trade Unions. Even the anti-internationalist Socialist Party of Norman Thomas finds it necessary to maintain its affiliation to the Labor and Socialist International, the "Second International."

The petty bourgeoisie itself was deeply influenced by the growth of internationalism, as is witnessed by such organizations as Rotary, Masonry, Kiwanis, and so forth. The Catholic Church has made its deepest appeal in the United States precisely upon the basis of its claims to universality, to transcending all national boundaries; and the Evangelical churches competed in this field, with their foreign missions, the international Y.M.C.A. and Y.W.C.A. and similar efforts.

There are various expressions of internationalism, some, progressive and revolutionary; others, of all shades of conservative and reactionary character. But there is only one consistent and complete internationalism today, and that is *proletarian internationalism,* the internationalism founded by Marx and Engels, and brought to its great, historically decisive victories under the leadership of Lenin and Stalin.

The best poets sang of "The brotherhood of man, the Federation of the World," as the highest social aspiration. This fundamental internationalism has always been at the heart of the best American tradition. This "Americanism" in its best manifestations has always been consciously in opposition to narrow nationalism and chauvinism. Internationalism is woven into the very fabric of American society and its history. From Thomas Jefferson, the passionate partisan of the French Revolution, and Thomas Paine, whose motto was: "The world is my country; to do good is my religion"; through Abraham Lincoln, and down to the modern labor movement; from Lafayette, von Steuben, Kosciusko, Pulaski, Schurz, Weydemeyer, down to the first draftees of the peace-time conscription of 1940—*internationalism* has always been an outstanding characteristic of Americanism.

It was as the inheritor of this great American tradition, as well as of the proletarian internationalism of Marx, Engels, and Lenin, that the Communist Party of the U. S. A. has from its birth lived and moved in the spirit of internationalism. It was in this great tradition that our Party was associated with, and finally affiliated to, the Communist International, that association of all the national Communist parties of the world.

Today we are faced with a law, but recently passed by Congress and signed by the President, the so-called "Voorhis Blacklist Act," which attempts by legalistic indirection to outlaw this principle of internationalism by placing intolerable penalties and burdens upon its organizational expression.

It is to consider the problems this Act raises for the Communist Party, and for this question alone, that our Special Convention has been called together.

HISTORICAL BACKGROUND OF THE VOORHIS ACT

The Voorhis Act comes as no surprise to us. It has an ancient, even if dishonorable, ancestry; it is nothing new in its essentials; it follows the established pattern of repression which the Party of Privilege and Reaction has used against the masses since the closing days of the eighteenth century in every great period of crisis, down to the present.

In the United States, the "family tree" of the Voorhis Act begins with the "Alien and Sedition Laws" of the Adams Administration, 1796-1800, which were directed against the rising Jeffersonian democracy. Jefferson became President in 1800, through the fight against these repressive laws, and against the reactionary social forces which raised these laws as their weapon against the people. The rising forces of democracy were denounced as "seditious," and their inspiration and leadership as "alien"; Jefferson was pictured as an "agent of the French Jacobins," while "French gold" was supposed to furnish the means of his struggle, and wonderfully enough in the light of today, the Society of Tammany in New York, one of the original "clubs" that organized Jefferson's rise to power, was denounced along with all its fellows as a "seditious conspiracy," directed by revolutionists abroad, by "foreign agents."

But the "Alien and Sedition Laws," inspired by Alexander Hamilton, the evil genius of the Adams Administration, failed to halt the march of history. The party of Jefferson came to power all the more surely and completely through its struggle against these laws, and the party which sponsored these laws, the Federalists, rapidly degenerated into cliques of traitorous conspirators, really agents of a foreign power, and disappeared from history with the stamp of treason indelibly upon it.

All modern versions of the "Alien and Sedition Laws" take their pattern from the Cologne Communist Trial, of the middle of the nineteenth century, with its chief figure, the infamous Police Chief Stieber, jobber in the forged evidence of provocateurs—the original Martin Dies—to prove a non-existent "international conspiracy"; from the France of the adventurer, Louis Napoleon, and Thiers; and from the "Anti-Socialist Laws" of the Germany of Bismarck.

The basic theory formulated and worked out in detail, and clung to ever since without change by the Party of Privilege and Reaction, is that the rise of labor as a political power within each nation is a "seditious conspiracy," always fomented by an "alien power" and the work of "foreign agents," the proof being the international character of the modern labor and Communist movements.

This theory reached its most complete development in the hands of Hitler, and by him was made the instrument whereby the British, French, and American bourgeoisies were enlisted to build up his power from nothing to where he felt able to challenge them all in a bold bid for world supremacy. Such is the depth and universality among the world bourgeoisie of the fears and the ideology behind the Voorhis Act.

One of the spiritual ancestors of the Voorhis Act was Allen Pinkerton, the man who was MacLellan's stool pigeon against Lincoln. This early ideologist of modern red-baiting against the labor movement put it bluntly and crudely when he wrote:

... Trade unions of every name and nature are but a relic of the old despotic days.... For years, and without any particular attention on the part of the press or the public, animated by the vicious dictatorships of the International Society, all manner of labor unions and leagues have been forming. No manufacturing town or city has escaped this baleful influence.

More immediate predecessors of the Voorhis Act were: the "Espionage Act" of 1917, under which Eugene Victor Debs was sent to prison; under which Victor Berger was deprived of his seat in Congress and sentenced to a long prison term, with others; under which Bill Haywood and scores of the I.W.W. leaders were convicted in mass trials and sentenced up to twenty years. Further, in the post-war years, there was the plague of "criminal syndicalism" laws in the states, under which occurred the Chicago and Bridgeman Communist cases, shamefacedly dropped during the "prosperity period" of the middle twenties; the Palmer "red-raids" and deportation hysteria of 1920, of which all decent Americans have been profoundly ashamed ever since. Of the same "family tree" was the expulsion of the New York Socialists from the State Legislature, an outrage which brought forth in protest even such a conservative as Charles Evans Hughes, then a prominent corporation lawyer and late Republican candidate for President against Wilson, and now Chief Justice of the Supreme Court.

Finally, to come to the latest period, the Voorhis Bill is the American application of Hitler's "Reichstag Fire Trial" of George Dimitroff at Leipzig. It is the codification of all the assaults legal, illegal, and extra legal, which have been made during the past year against the Communist Party and its leadership, by the Roosevelt Administration—an Administration which over previous years had gladly accepted Communist aid and support, which held power in New York only by that margin of votes cast for them by the Communists, and which solicited the continuance of such support even as late as July, 1940! It is an inevitable expression of policy by a bourgeoisie, and its leading party and President, which has set its course, stubbornly and reckless of consequences, into the very vortex of the imperialist war for the redivision of the world, against the will of labor and the vast majority of the American masses.

This is the historical background, this is the "family tree," of the Voorhis Act, which has now become "the law of the land."

PROVISIONS AND CONSEQUENCES OF THE VOORHIS ACT

Under the mask of identifying and regulating organizations having a criminal character or tendency (for which no new laws are conceivably necessary, all crimes being fully covered by existing laws), the Voorhis Act reaches its real object when it brings under its penalties and provisions all organizations "subject to foreign control," and then defines such "foreign control" as inclusive of any affiliation that reaches beyond the boundaries of the United States. The Communist Party is not under any form of foreign control, but it does have international affiliation, and thereby is classified by this Act as under "foreign control."

From the clear provisions of the Act, then, *every organization* which has any affiliation in another country is subject to its provisions and penalties. A list of such organizations would include, first of all, the American Federation of Labor as a whole, with every affiliate, for the A. F. of L., in addition to its branches in Canada and connections in Latin America, is an important affiliate to the International Federation of Trade Unions, the so-called "Amsterdam

International." It would not include, curiously enough, the Congress of Industrial Organizations (C.I.O.), except those of its affiliates which themselves have branches in Canada. It would include the American Legion, the Veterans of Foreign Wars, and other ex-soldier organizations, practically all of which have international tie-ups. It would include the Y.M.C.A., the Y.W.C.A., the Young Hebrews, the Zionists, etc., for while religious organizations are specifically exempt, such social and political organizations with religious colorings and tendencies are not. It would, of course, include the Socialist Party, the Social-Democrats and smaller political groupings. It would include Rotary, Masonry, Kiwanis, various sport and cultural organizations, including the Amateur Athletic Association, philatelic and numismatic associations, all of which are not purely scientific in the narrow sense. A very broad net, indeed, is cast by the Voorhis Act.

Is such a big haul, as here indicated, the immediate object of the Act? No, indeed not. Such complete imitation of Hitlerism is not practical for the moment; that is only the "poetry of the future." The chief, if not the only, immediate objective of the Act is the Communist Party. How, then, will its broad and all-inclusive net be manipulated to catch this one little fish and let the big ones through?

The answer is found in the provision which places every question of the application of the Act at *the discretion of the Attorney General*. The act in practice applies *to no one and to no organization,* unless and until the Attorney General, in his discretion, so proclaims. Absolute and unrestrained power is conferred upon the Attorney General to decide who comes under the provisions of the Act, when, and in what manner. There is not even any pretense of judicial review, except as to application of penalties. How the discretion of Attorneys General is exercised in such questions, we already have received ample demonstration during the past fourteen months.

There cannot be the slightest doubt that the Communist Party would in the beginning be the chief if not the sole object of attention;

only later would the broad mass organizations feel the direct blows of the Act. This conclusion is also borne out by our observation of what has happened in other lands; the fate being prepared for the people is always first inflicted upon the Communists.

Now, when the Attorney General has exercised his discretion and applies the Act to a particular organization, what are the consequences? Here, again, the Act in application is just as flexible as the discretion of the Attorney General; it can be a mere formality, or it can run whatever gamut of severity may be imagined. At the Attorney General's discretion, it may require the designated organization and its officers to file with the Attorney General a complete list of names and addresses of each and every *member and supporter,* the address of every meeting prior to its occurrence, complete accounting of all money gathered and used directly or indirectly in furtherance of the organization's work, copies of every item of printed or mimeographed material issued or inspired by the organization or its officers. These provisions apply to every unit of the organization and every official, from the top down to the smallest local branch or committee. Each and every separate instance of failure to comply with the discretionary demands of the Attorney General renders each and every person responsible therefor subject to imprisonment for a term up to five years, and a fine up to $5,000.

Clearly it is impossible for any organization subjected to the provisions of this Act to operate at all except with the *benevolent discretion* of the Attorney General of the United States. Any organization brought under its provisions would be absolutely at the mercy of that official. It would first of all have to establish, by its own action, such a blacklist of its members and supporters as Martin Dies has been working on for years, at the disposal of all its worst enemies. Secondly, it could not, even if it wished, furnish every report that might be required of it, without halting all normal operations of the organization, and would therefore automatically be subject to a pyramiding of penalties *at the discretion of the At-*

torney General. All of which is merely a masked form of outlawing such organizations as may be chosen by administrative edict.

The Voorhis Act is therefore an extreme example of the most vicious and oppressive Exceptional Laws. Under its smooth camouflage lie the sharp claws of fascism. It is the most dangerous blow yet dealt at the remnants of American democracy. It is an attempt, under cover of war hysteria, to outlaw that principle of internationalism which Abraham Lincoln said was the strongest bond of human sympathy outside of the family, a principle which flows out of the deepest loyalty to the masses of our own nation, and which is put so truly and beautifully in the following words of Mark Twain's *Connecticut Yankee:*

You see, my kind of loyalty was loyalty to one's country, not to its institutions or its office holders. The country is the real thing, the substantial thing, the eternal thing; it is the thing to watch over, and care for, and be loyal to; institutions are extraneous, they are its mere clothing, and clothing can wear out, become ragged, cease to be comfortable, cease to protect the body from winter, disease, death. To be loyal to rags, to shout for rags, to worship rags—that is loyalty to unreason, it is pure animal; it belongs to monarchy, was invented by monarchy; let monarchy keep it. I was from Connecticut, whose Constitution declares: "that all political power is inherent in the people, and all free governments are founded on their authority and instituted for their benefit; and that they have at all times an undeniable and indefeasible right to alter their form of government in such manner as they may think expedient."

Under that gospel, the citizen who thinks he sees that the commonwealth's political clothes are worn out, and yet holds his peace and does not agitate for a new suit, is disloyal; he is a traitor. That he may be the only one who thinks he sees this decay, does not excuse him; it is his duty to agitate anyway, and it is the duty of others to vote him down if they do not see the matter as he does.*

How Can the Communist Party Meet the Voorhis Act?

Under present conditions it is impossible for the Communist Party to operate under the provisions of the Voorhis Act. An

* Mark Twain, *A Connecticut Yankee in King Arthur's Court,* p. 107, New York, 1917.

intensely hostile Administration, which already has not hesitated to go outside the law to try to crush us, can certainly not be expected to exercise its arbitrary discretion with the slightest leniency. The courts will be debarred by the Act from exercising any restraining influence, even assuming an independent and freedom-loving judiciary, which is a bold assumption today, for *the single and admitted fact of international affiliation* removes all judicial discretion and makes administrative discretion absolute. The only way judicial relief could be found at all would be through attacking the constitutionality of the Act. While the Act is clearly unconstitutional, the possible establishment of that fact by judicial process, up to the Supreme Court, after some years, offers not the slightest hope of relief in the critically important period just ahead.

Henry Ford and Tom Girdler, with many others of their kind, are able calmly to defy the most definite and constitutional laws of the land over many years, do it successfully, and be rewarded with rich, fat Government contracts and swollen profits. It would be somewhat over-optimistic to expect that the Communist Party could ignore the Voorhis Act with even the smallest fraction of the success that attends Ford, Girdler & Co. in defying the labor laws. To ignore or defy the Voorhis Act will in all probability result in the same sort of outlawing and hunting down of Communists, which in France was done directly without any camouflage as the prelude to the shameful and catastrophic capitulation of that country to the Nazi invasion.

If the time comes when the American people and the American Communists cannot avoid going through an American variant of the French tragedy, we Communists of the New World will not flinch from the test. We can feel calmly confident that we will uphold the high honor of proletarian internationalism in the spirit and tradition of our national heroes, Jefferson, Paine, Lincoln, Debs, Ruthenberg, Haywood, and the higher spirit and tradition of our international teachers and exemplars, Marx, Engels, Lenin, and Stalin, of the Russian Bolsheviks, of George Dimitroff, of the Spanish, Chinese, German, French, of the best Communists of all the

world. American Communists will always have the qualities necessary to keep the name of our country high on the international
honor roll.

Does the Voorhis Act represent such a definitive fascization of
America that it leaves the Communist Party no choice but capitulation or being considered illegal? That it may be made to represent
such a development, by administrative edict, is clear. But a careful
examination of the question will cause us to withhold such a conclusion until it is forced upon us.

First, we have witnessed the example of England where, after
more than fourteen months of war and several months of horrible
bombardments from the air, the Communist Party of Great Britain
still functions as a legal party, with a member of Parliament, Willie
Gallacher; the war hysteria has not overwhelmed it into illegality,
despite all the restrictions of wartime under a bourgeois government.
While it is true that the American bourgeoisie is more hysterical,
more jittery, than the British, even with the war three thousand
miles away and our country still "non-belligerent," yet we may still
keep the door open for possible restraining influences to operate, to
keep America from the full measure of fascization which threatens.
We are not forced to anticipate illegalization of our Party in the
immediate future from general considerations.

Secondly, as to the Voorhis Act itself, it has the peculiarity that
it avoids the direct attack upon political opinions, principles and
teachings, in so far as anything applying to the Communist Party
is concerned. We are not advocates of force and violence, we are not
foreign agents, we are not under any foreign control—nothing whatever in the Voorhis Act brings the Communist Party under its provisions except the single fact of *international affiliation*—our formal
adherence to the Communist International as an organized part of
a world party.

This affiliation is the formal organizational expression of the
principle of proletarian internationalism, a principle to which the
life of every Communist is unconditionally consecrated. For this
principle we will whenever necessary gladly give our lives, for it is

that which gives life meaning, makes it proud, heroic, worth living, the only guarantee for the whole future of humanity.

Can we consider taking the step of dissolving the formal, official affiliation of the Communist Party of the U. S. A. to the Communist International as the only way to avoid immediate practical illegalization of our Party under the Voorhis Act? Must we defend this concrete organizational expression of our fundamental principle in the same unconditional, uncompromising way we defend and always will defend the principle itself?

Our National Committee has been giving its most profound and heart-searching thought to this question. If such a step should be in any way a surrender to, or a strengthening of, any tendencies to surrender or weaken among the broad membership of our Party, we would reject the step of disaffiliation at once, without hesitation. If such a step should cause us to waver, to vacillate, in the carrying of the full message of proletarian internationalism to the broadest masses of American workers, we would condemn it out of hand without further thought.

Proletarian internationalism, the development of a common understanding of their problems of life and peace by the workers and toiling masses of every country, overriding all national boundaries, and out of this common understanding the forging of common and interrelated policies and action—this is the only road out of the bloody catastrophe of the imperialist war, this is the only way to peace, this is the only road to the future for humanity.

Can the Communist Party of the U. S. A. fight most effectively for this principle under the conditions of a continued, though harassed and precarious, legality, bought at the price of a temporary and unwilling dissolution of the immediate and present international affiliation with our brother parties in the Communist International? Or can we fight most effectively by defying this shameful, reactionary, and unconstitutional law and accept whatever consequences may flow from such a course?

Our National Committee has called this Special Convention to put the question before the supreme authority of our Party. At our

Eleventh National Convention you delegated full power to the National Committee, or to its Political Committee, to make any change in the Party Constitution that might be required to defend the legality of the Party. This question is so vital that we decided not to exercise this authority without putting the question again to a fully representative convention.

The National Committee submits to you, for your decision, a definite recommendation:

That the Communist Party of the U. S. A., in Convention assembled, does hereby cancel and dissolve its organizational affiliation to the Communist International, as well as any and all other bodies of any kind outside the boundaries of the United States of America, for the specific purpose of removing itself from the terms of the so-called Voorhis Act, which originated in the House of Representatives as H. R. 10094, which has been enacted and goes into effect in January, 1941, which law would otherwise tend to destroy, and would destroy, the position of the Communist Party as a legal and open political party of the American working class;

That the Convention denounces the Voorhis Act as harmful and destructive of the democratic rights of the people, as designed to coerce the people into submission to the entry of the United States into the imperialist war, and as a part of the sweep of fascization over the capitalist world;

That the Convention pledges the Party to work untiringly to secure the repeal of this law, to the end that labor and our Party shall be secure and unmolested in its sacred rights of international affiliation of all workers, which in the words of Lincoln express "the strongest bond of human sympathy outside of the family relationship";

That the Convention reaffirms the unshakable adherence of our Party to the principles of proletarian internationalism, in the spirit of its greatest leaders and teachers, Marx, Engels, Lenin and Stalin, which offer the only road to the future for suffering humanity;

That the Convention formally and officially declares that the Communist Party of the United States is responsible for no political document, policy, book, article, or other expression of political opinion, except such as are issued by itself, through its regularly constituted leadership, on the basis of the Eleventh National Convention deliberations and decisions, and of this present Special Convention;

That the Convention does now select a sub-committee to consider the Constitution and By-Laws of the Communist Party of the U. S. A., as adopted at the Tenth National Convention, and bring back to this Convention its recommendations for such amendments, changes, or deletions, which shall most effectively express these basic decisions in such Constitution and By-Laws.

Report to the Emergency National Convention of the Communist Party, New York, November 16, 1940.

II. A YEAR IN REVIEW

ANOTHER year is over. It was a momentous year, in which history was speeded-up as never before. So many things happened that we may not be able to see the forest for the trees, may overlook the most important things. Therefore the value of a review at the moment when 1940 changes over to 1941.

Outstanding development of the year is that the imperialist war has spread to involve practically the entire world—except the Union of Soviet Socialist Republics. The capitalist and the colonial or semi-colonial countries are, with a few unimportant exceptions, fully in the storm of the most destructive, most catastrophic struggle of all history. This is clearly the deepest crisis of the capitalist world system.

The most important net result of the year, on a world scale, has been the shift in the relation of forces as between the capitalist world, on the one hand, and the new socialist world of the U.S.S.R., on the other hand, a shift in favor of the Soviet Union of great magnitude as yet immeasurable. This is irrefutably established by the addition of six new Soviet republics comprising some twenty-three million inhabitants to the Soviet Union, and by the removal of the Mannerheim Line from the neck of Leningrad. The capitalist world has a net loss which includes further the gigantic destruction of its war.

The United States has, during 1940, been deeply involved in the imperialist war. At the beginning of the year, the U.S.A. could still be described as a neutral (though that neutrality was already being undermined), outside the orbit of the war. But in the very midst of the national elections, fought between two parties which both protested their firmest intention of keeping out of the war, our Government was irretrievably committed to the deepest involvement, in flagrant violation of even the pretense of democratic forms. Upon this judgment, the Communists find themselves in agreement with the most sober and realistic spokesmen of the ruling class (when the latter are talking among themselves, and not to the masses).

The President of the National Industrial Conference Board, Virgil Jordan, speaking to the Convention of the Investment Bankers' Association on December 10 revealed the true mind of America's rulers, in a speech which merits repeated quotation. He said:

Whatever the facts about this war may have been or are now, it must be unmistakably clear to any intelligent person that we are engaged in it.

This decisive fact is still concealed from the masses of the people. Mr. Jordan explained the reason for this to the bankers in words that fully confirm Lenin's exposure of imperialism in the last war. He said:

In peace time it is the accepted custom and normal manners of modern government to conceal all important facts from the public, or to lie about them; in war it is a political vice which becomes a public necessity. ... People in every country, including our own ... [are] treated as though they were helpless wards or incompetent inmates of some vast institution for the indigent and feeble-minded. It is in much this spirit and atmosphere that the chatter and prattle about our national defense program proceeds in this country today.

Only one correction is needed to this description. It applies to capitalist, imperialist governments. The Union of Soviet Socialist Republics has spoken to its own people and to the world in the most frank and realistic terms, has told the naked truth.

The reactionary imperialistic character of the war has been revealed, in 1940, to all but dunces, ignoramuses, and those who refuse to see. Mr. Jordan described it for the bankers in terms which every worker should study again and again. He said:

Even the job of winning the war, with England or alone, is only part of the task to which America has committed herself for the future. Whatever the outcome of the war, America has embarked upon a career of imperialism, both in world affairs and in every other aspect of her life.... Even though, by our aid, England should emerge from this struggle without defeat, she will be so impoverished economically and crippled in prestige that it is improbable she will be able to resume or maintain the dominant position in world affairs which she has occupied so long. At best, England will become a junior partner in a new Anglo-Saxon imperialism, in which the economic resources and the military and naval strength of the United States will be the center of gravity. Southward in our hemisphere and westward in the Pacific the path of empire takes its way, and in modern terms of economic power as well as political prestige, the sceptre passes to the United States.

All this is what lies beneath the phrase "national defense"—some of it deeply hidden, some of it very near the surface and soon to emerge to challenge us.

And what does all this mean for 1941? Impoverishment of the American people, for the enrichment of American bankers on a scale unprecedented in history. We Communists have predicted and described this imperialism in our own terms, but again I prefer to turn to Mr. Jordan, the expert adviser of the bankers. After noting "the suffering and destruction involved in war, and the economic depression and political disturbance which almost invariably follow it," Mr. Jordan warns the bankers to stop thinking of the war "as a vast wasteful expenditure and a grinding burden on the community," for it will be "most helpful" he says, to "conceive of this commitment in the most constructive terms, as a kind of vast investment."

Vast indeed is to be this "investment" in empire. Mr. Jordan describes the most probable sources from which will be drawn this investment:

Recent studies by the Conference Board indicate that, even if we were to be spending or investing as much as fifteen billion a year on armaments, as we did during a full year of the last World War, we could squeeze that much or more out of the consumption and savings of the community at the current national income level. . . . However it is made, everyone in the community must consciously or unconsciously participate in this investment . . . even the unemployed, whether they know it or not.

That is the conception that guides the American ruling class, the bourgeoisie and its government in Washington. The collapse and disintegration of the world capitalist system, the carnage and catastrophe of the imperialist war—all this they see chiefly as a "golden opportunity" for American monopoly capital, American imperialism, to come into its inheritance, a sort of glorified "fire sale" in which they will seize and buy up the world cheaply.

But they make their plans without sufficient consideration of the American working class, the American people. The American masses have different aspirations and ideas, not represented by a Sidney Hillman. The ruling class has taken the nation on the "path of empire" only by the most brazen and cynical deception.

As they awaken to the truth the American masses will brush those plans aside.

Let 1941 be the year of the great awakening!

Sunday Worker, *December 29, 1940.*

III. FREE LUIS CARLOS PRESTES

ALL true anti-imperialists throughout the Americas will today greet Luis Carlos Prestes on his forty-third birthday as the outstanding symbol of the struggle of the colonial and semi-colonial peoples of this hemisphere for national liberation from imperialist oppression.

Today when our own American ruling class is desperately trying to drag our country into the present imperialist war and is carrying through a policy of economic and political aggrandizement aimed at the further subjugation of the peoples and nations of this hemisphere, the struggle to liberate Luis Carlos Prestes becomes an integral part of the fight for freedom, peace and against imperialist war.

For leading the struggle to liberate his people, Luis Carlos Prestes was sentenced in 1935 to sixteen years' imprisonment. The Vargas dictatorship acting under pressure of the imperialist war-makers and of our own Government, unable to suppress the deep ferment prevailing within the country, and enormous sympathy that the Brazilian people manifest towards Prestes, brought him to trial again in an attempt, through this attack against his life, to further terrorize and enslave the people of Brazil.

The conduct of Prestes before the Vargas "justice," where his life was at stake, is an admirable example of his greatness as a leader of the people. Facing his enemies and the enemies of his country—after being held in jail for more than five years—Prestes used this only opportunity to appeal to his people, encouraging them to unite and to follow the example of the great October Revolution as the only path that can lead to their final liberation.

We Americans can truly be proud of such a great leader and liberator. We must continue the fight for Prestes' freedom and for amnesty to all political prisoners in Brazil. By so doing we will be cementing the bonds that will unite the people of Brazil and America into a solid front against imperialism.

Daily Worker, *January 3, 1941.*

IV. THE WAY OUT OF THE
   IMPERIALIST WAR

LENIN died seventeen years ago. But his spirit lives as the beloved teacher and guide of tens of millions in all lands, because he and his party alone showed the way out of the last imperialist war, the way to peace and socialism.

Today, in the midst of the second imperialist war, we commemorate Lenin by applying his teachings in order fully to understand and master the problems raised by this continuation of the first World War.

The first requirement for understanding our problems is to face facts as they are, however unpleasant. And it is a fact, unpleasant indeed, that America *is in the war*. Most of the current newspaper and radio chatter about keeping out of the war is merely to hide a while longer the fact that we are already in it, that our problem is: "What way out?"

President Roosevelt has submitted to Congress what is called a "defense budget" of seventeen-and-a-half billion dollars, with more to come. It is for defense only in a very special sense that it is a "defense" of the ambitions of Wall Street, of the "sixty families," to extend their power over the world in a new empire—"the mightiest empire the world has ever seen."

The President told Congress that his aim is to bring his conception of "liberty" to "the entire world." That the aim of the gigantic war budget extends to the entire world is not to be questioned. But the quality of the "liberty" involved is more doubtful. That "liberty" is best characterized by the status of the three hundred and fifty million British subjects in India, whose erstwhile ruler, Lord Halifax, is on his way to Washington to represent "our ally," the British Empire, bearing with him, according to the word of Winston Churchill, all the most intimate secrets of the war aims, which we common people may hope that our children may some day also learn. Or even the "liberty" of our own Solid South, where the vote is the monopoly of some ten to twenty per cent of the population, where Judge Lynch holds sway.

War Aims of American Imperialism

Woodrow Wilson in the last war covered up American imperialism's war aims with similar idealistic chatter. Only he was more modest, corresponding to the more modest role of Wall Street in the world at that time. He only wanted to "make the world safe for democracy." Roosevelt proposes to take his brand of democracy—with Winston Churchill's—and make it supreme over the whole world.

But the extension of American or British control over the whole world is not democracy. It is imperialism. It is a proposal to abolish American democracy at home and spread the control of the "sixty families" of an American banking and industrial oligarchy over all the world. It is a big order, indeed, and seventeen-and-a-half billion dollars is none too much as the current down-payment. It will surely cost a hundred times that before the adventure is closed —in dollars and millions in lives of the American people.

The Roosevelt Administration has entered into a compact to aid the British ruling class to retain control of a slave empire in half of Africa, to continue to rule three hundred and fifty million Indians against their will. The Roosevelt Administration is about to enter into military action which cannot but be directed against Ireland. It is now adding its pressure to that of Churchill and Halifax to compel Ireland to surrender its natural fortifications again to the British Government. We Americans do not wish to have our country made an instrument of war to aid the British rulers to renew and complete the conquest of Ireland that they have unsuccessfully attempted for seven hundred years.

The war administration of Roosevelt arrogates to itself the right to enclose the whole hemisphere in its control. It is scarcely concealed as a plan to fasten upon twenty Latin American republics the relationship to the United States that India has to Great Britain. Already the Roosevelt Administration presumes to dispute the right of Latin American republics to control their own foreign trade or to regulate their relations with other nations independently of the Washington State Department. This is not democracy. This is imperialism. It is an assault, behind the smooth words of diplomacy, against the sovereignty of twenty heroic independent Latin American nations which we declare will never submit to this conquest.

The true measure of Roosevelt's idealistic demagogy, and of American democracy in general, may be found in the words of Virgil Jordan, speaking to the Bankers' Association last month, an oft-quoted paragraph which will bear many repetitions. It is, as the saying goes, "right out of the horse's mouth"; it comes from the highest circles of our ruling class. Allow me to repeat Mr. Jordan's revelation:

In peace time it is the accepted custom and normal manners of modern government to conceal all important facts from the public, or to lie about them; in war it is a political vice which becomes a public necessity. . . . People in every country, including our own . . . [are] treated as though they were helpless wards or incompetent inmates of some vast institution for the indigent and feeble-minded. It is in much this spirit and atmosphere that the chatter and prattle about our national defense program proceeds in this country today.

Yes, America is in the imperialist war, for imperialist aims, despite all the chatter and prattle about "liberty" and "democracy" and other nice things, and despite the illusion that it is still a matter for debate as to whether "we shall go in."

There are still a few Congressmen who seem to think that Congress has something to say about it. They are dreaming of the past.

Congress abdicated its powers last September, when it gave silent consent to Roosevelt's coup d'état of the destroyers-bases deal, the date of which, September 3, will probably be taken by future historians to mark United States' entrance into the war. Roosevelt already has seized and exercised all the powers that Congress debates giving him; Congress has left for itself no role but that of voting "Ja."

The masses of the people were overwhelmingly and consciously opposed to America's entrance into the war. This overwhelming will to peace was so strong that, during the election campaign, it forced even Roosevelt and Willkie to bow to it, to make hypocritical promises to respect it. That was accomplished by the Hitlerian tactic of concentrating upon a single step at a time, by swearing to high heaven that each step was the last one, by telling lies so big and bold that little people feared to question them.

Thus the American people are placed in a position in many respects similar to that of the German people: both were against the war, both were thrown in by their rulers without their consent, both have lost whatever traditional checks they may have had upon their rulers, both must seek a way out of the war in spite and against the will of their present rulers.

Fascism or Nazism is merely the military rule, the open terroristic dictatorship, or monopoly capital in its final stages of decay, and it becomes approximately the same in character in every capitalist country. Our own country is leveling itself with Germany in this respect even more swiftly than Britain.

SOCIAL-DEMOCRACY BEATS THE DRUMS

Our own "liberals" and Social-Democrats are beating the drums most loudly for the imperialist war. They deny most vehemently, of course, that it is an imperialist war. But the *Nation,* the *New Republic,* and other idealistic whitewashers of the imperialist war, who wish to "sell" the war to the people entirely ignore such things as the programmatic speech of Mr. Jordan to the Bankers' Convention. That proves they belong, not among the deceived, but among the deceivers. If they were honest, they would print Mr. Jordan's speech and try to refute it. But they dare not try it; the country would know that Mr. Jordan is much closer to the seats of power than are the "liberals." They therefore simply ignore, and do not try to answer, such revelations as the following from Mr. Jordan, which should be repeated again and again until it has penetrated the mind of every American worker:

Whatever the outcome of the war, America has embarked upon a career of imperialism, both in world affairs and in every other aspect of life here.... At best, England will become a junior partner in a new Anglo-Saxon imperialism, in which...the United States will be the center of gravity. Southward in our hemisphere and westward in the Pacific the path of empire takes its way...the scepter passes to the United States. All this is what lies beneath the phrase "national defense"—some of it deeply hidden, some of it very near the surface and soon to emerge to challenge us.

The forces that drag the capitalist countries one after another into the war arise from the very nature of the capitalist system, which in its monopolist phase of today, the stage of parasitism and decay, is incompatible with an expanding and peaceful life for the people of any country which it rules. It is capitalism itself that drives to war, and now that the war has been unleashed to the extent of involving practically the entire capitalist world, it is clear that the downfall of capitalism itself is involved in the problem of peace. There is no way out of the war except in the popular resistance to the rule of the war-makers who have involved their whole system of imperialism so deeply that even they now admit that peace cannot again come to the world without their overthrow. It is a veiled admission that the socialist revolution, the coming to power of the working class, is the alternative to unlimited slaughter and enslavement.

Because we Communists proclaim this truth, because we explain it in all its detail, as Lenin did during the last World War, we are being denounced as "traitors," as "conspirators," as "agents of a foreign power." This is based upon the theory that "patriots" are only those who loyally serve monopoly capital, Wall Street, the economic royalists—and Communists certainly do not; are only those who agree and help put into effect the policies which bring upon our country the devastation of war—and the Communists certainly do not; are only those who help tie America up with one side in the imperialist war—and Communists certainly do not. We Communists are patriots of a different sort; we would serve the country we love by keeping it at peace, by maintaining strict neutrality toward the imperialist war, by freeing it from the yoke of monopoly capital.

The absurd lie is spread against us that we Communists conspire to commit sabotage and "fifth column" work to achieve our ends. What nonsense this is! Such methods are not ours. Why should we dream that any puny efforts of a few individuals at destruction could have any importance in a world where the monster powers of the capitalist governments are devoted to destruction on the most gigantic scale? We are not such fools. The destruction of the capitalist world is being carried out under the direction of Hitler and Churchill, of Mussolini and Petain, of Franco and the Mikado —and now of Roosevelt. We Communists are not entering into that competition. We have other work to do, to explain to the masses the reasons behind all this senseless destruction and disaster, to show them the way out of this chaos, to prepare them for the construction of the new world—the world of socialism, of the common ownership of the country's economy and its operation by and for the masses of the people. As old Wilhelm Liebknecht answered the Kaiser's court in 1872, replying to similar charges, we Communists conspire only in the open, as the sun conspires against darkness and night.

The Way Out of the War

What then is the way out of the war? Look back at the last World War! The nations were locked in the embrace of mutual destruction, and the ruling classes of none of them could point any way out except to complete the destruction. Peace came only when the masses, the workers, peasants and soldiers, of one great country, Russia, took their fate into their own hands, overthrew the old rulers, proclaimed socialism and peace. They were threatened with the most dire consequences. The Kaiser's Germany forced a victor's peace at Brest Litovsk—but the people of Germany soon overthrew the Kaiser in a revolution of their own. The United States, Britain, France, Japan made an undeclared war against them—but the peoples stirred against their own governments, and forced them to withdraw. The Russian Revolution in 1917, under the leadership of Lenin and Stalin, brought the end of the last World War.

The present imperialist world war will be brought to an end by a similar revolution in one or more of the major countries of Europe. It cannot be ended by the present rulers, but only by their overthrow. The peoples themselves must end this war.

Those whose first and only loyalty is to capitalism, to the little group of rich families who own most of the nation's basic economy, cry out that this is "treason." But the world has seen, in country after country, that it is precisely the capitalists and their agents who betray their country, who will make any kind of abject surrender to foreign powers whenever they find it impossible otherwise to keep their own people in subjection, to keep possession of their profits. The real traitors in every nation are those who put the profits of finance capital as their first consideration. And these are the present rulers in all capitalist countries.

Not so long ago, some of these basic truths, now labeled "treason" by the warmongers, had such wide acceptance that even President Roosevelt repeated them in his speeches. It is very interesting today to quote some past utterances of the leader of the war party.

. . . We could get a world accord on world peace immediately if the people of the world could speak for themselves. Through all the centuries of recorded history and down to the world conflict of 1914 to 1918, wars were made by governments. . . . They [the people] wondered . . . whether the people themselves could not some day prevent governments from making war . . . to propose in this newer generation that from now on war by governments shall be changed to peace by peoples. (December 28, 1933.)

... The United States ... can play but one role; through a well-ordered neutrality to do naught to encourage the contest; through adequate defense to save ourselves from ... attack; and through example ... to persuade other nations to return to the ways of peace. ... (January 3, 1936.)

... It is clear to me that greatly to exceed that basis [of normal peace-time exports], with the result of earning profits not possible during peace, and especially with the result of giving actual assistance to the carrying on of war, would serve to magnify the very evil of war which we seek to prevent. (February 29, 1936.)

... Industrial and agricultural production for a war market may give immense fortunes to a few men; for the nation as a whole it produces disaster. ... It was the prospect of war profits that caused the extension of monopoly and unjustified expansion of industry and a price level so high that the normal relationship between debtor and creditor was destroyed. Nevertheless, if war should break out again in another continent, let us not blink the fact that we would find in this country thousands of Americans who, seeking immediate riches—fools' gold—would attempt to break down or evade our neutrality.

They would tell you—and, unfortunately, their views would get wide publicity—that if they could produce and ship this and that and the other article to belligerent nations, the unemployed of America would all find work. They would tell you that if they could extend credit to warring nations that credit would be used in the United States to build homes and factories and pay our debts. They would tell you that America would once more capture the trade of the world.

It would be hard to resist that clamor; it would be hard for many Americans, I fear, to look beyond—to realize the inevitable penalties, the inevitable day of reckoning, that come from false prosperity. To resist the clamor of that greed, if war should come, would require the unswerving support of all Americans who love peace (August 14, 1936.)

... Vast armaments are rising on every side and ... the work of creating them employs men and women by the millions. ... Such employment is false employment; ... it builds no permanent structures and creates no consumers' goods for the maintenance of lasting prosperity. We know that nations guilty of these follies inevitably face the day when either their weapons of destruction must be used against their neighbors or when an unsound economy, like a house of cards, will fall apart. (December 1, 1936.)

Those words were profoundly true when they were spoken; they are a thousand times true today. But the man who uttered them was himself unable to "resist that clamor." Step by step he has violated every warning he himself uttered, until he is the unchallenged head of the greatest war dictatorship the world has ever seen. He is piling up for the United States and all the Americas those "inevitable penalties," that "inevitable day of reckoning," the chaos and collapse that have already engulfed Europe and a large part of Asia and Africa.

Because the Communists have stood firm, have resisted the clamor of that greed, have stood unswerving with "all Americans who love peace" and with the lovers of peace in all lands, especially the great stronghold of peace, the Union of Soviet Socialist Republics—that is the reason why the Communists are being persecuted with exceptional legislation, that is why all real progressives and lovers of peace are being labeled "Communists" and included in the persecution, all according to the formula which Hitler used for his rise to power.

It is for the realization of the aim that "war by governments shall be changed to peace by peoples," that the great People's Convention gathered in London over this last week end. We join with all peace-loving people everywhere in greeting that Convention and hailing its great work, which shows the way for the people of all belligerent countries, for the people of the suffering world.

The constant and increasing struggle for labor organization, for higher wages, shorter hours, and better working conditions, is the most essential foundation also of the struggle for peace, and to defeat every new step to take us deeper into the war. It goes hand in hand with the unrelenting battle to preserve and extend popular democratic rights and civil liberties, for preserving public education from the warmongers and red baiters, for a democratic people's culture.

But it must be recognized that the destruction of these democratic rights is an inseparable part of the Roosevelt "power" bill; it is a proposal for the overthrow of the republican form of government set up by Washington and Jefferson, and defended now, not by the Republican and Democratic parties, but only by the workers and farmers, by the masses.

The Peace Policy of the Soviet Union

These things are not lost, however, because our rulers have plunged our country into the war; they are merely under more fierce attack than ever before; they can never be lost except the masses give up their fight for them. And it is my firm conviction that the American workers will never give up that fight.

The year 1941 differs from 1917 in many respects. The greatest difference is that today the greatest power in the world is the socialist Soviet Union, that it is outside the orbit of the imperialist war and will not participate in it on one or the other side, that it is pursuing a consistent policy for peace for itself and for the whole world. The foundation for this great stronghold of peace is the magnificently successful building of the new socialist society, which rises to new heights of achievement at the moment when the capitalist world descends into a welter of blood and destruction. This great power, the U.S.S.R., is the embodiment of the rule of the people, of the working class, of the masses, in every phase of life. It is a democracy infinitely higher than anything even dreamed of before. It is the realization of the teachings of Lenin, and of his great and wise successor and continuator, Stalin. It is the guarantee of the ultimate attainment of peace and democracy in spite of the war-makers, of the abolition of capitalist exploitation, from which war arises, of the liberation of all humanity from all oppression. It is the living example of the path out of the imperialist war to a life of well being and peace, which all the world will ultimately follow.

Speech delivered at the Lenin Memorial meeting, Madison Square Garden, January 13, 1941.

V. CONTRADICTIONS IN WASHINGTON'S IMPERIALIST FOREIGN POLICY

WHAT is the fateful inner compulsion which drives imperialist statesmen along upon self-defeating and catastrophic paths?

The answer is that they hold fast to aims which are contradictory, which are mutually exclusive, but neither of which they, as imperialists, can abandon. Their policy always contains contradictory elements. They suffer from inner contradictions.

The outstanding example in all history of this characteristic feature of imperialism was the notorious Chamberlain policy of the British ruling class with its culmination at Munich and its collapse in September, 1939, the policy of "appeasement" which blew up in the hands of its makers.

But the same sort of contradictions exist and operate in every imperialist policy, whatever its name or form. They exist and operate in Roosevelt's current policies in foreign affairs.

It is the purpose of this article to examine these inner contradictions as they work out in life in some of the current applications of Washington's foreign policy. The existence of these contradictions is the conclusive evidence that United States participation in the war is for imperialistic aims.

AMERICA'S SELF-DEFEATING POLICY TOWARD CHINA

A few days ago the *New York Herald Tribune* carried a dispatch from its Far Eastern correspondent, Edgar Snow, describing certain inner developments within the Chinese republic which threatened its unity and raised the danger of its collapse and capitulation to the Japanese invaders. This was so disturbing to U. S. official circles that in order to reassure them the Chinese Consul in New York, after cabling his Government, addressed all New York newspapers with a letter denying there exists any rift in the unity of the Chinese people.

This incident seems to show that U. S. imperialists desire the unity of the Chinese republic, at least in so far as this is necessary for it to continue resistance to the Japanese invasion. But at the same time, it is a known and established fact that Washington encourages, stimulates, and strengthens the "anti-Communist" influences in the Chinese republic, whose activities had given rise to the dangers reported by Snow. Washington desires, at one and the same time, the annihilation of the Chinese Communists and the unity of the Chinese people against the Japanese invaders.

These two aims are contradictory; they cancel out each other. Chinese resistance to the invasion *began* with the re-establishment of the united front between the Kuomintang and the Chinese Communist Party. It will collapse, so far as the Chungking Government is concerned, if and when that united front is broken. The Chinese Communist Party has made the most costly sacrifices to maintain that united front; but within the Kuomintang all those who take their policy from U. S. and British influences *are agreed with those who wish capitulation to Japan* that the united front should be broken up. Washington's anti-Communist policy within the U. S. is carried over into its Chinese policy, and it weakens, undermines and defeats the aim to sustain the resistance of the Chinese Republic.

Edgar Snow's dispatch revealed these facts clearly to the careful reader. He warned of the danger of a rift and civil war, and at the same time he revealed that this danger arose *after* the United States had granted a loan to Chungking, and *as a result* of this fact.

For years the Soviet Union has been giving Chungking large loans and military supplies, compared with which all other outside help, including American, has been small, only a fraction of the Soviet aid. The Chinese republic has existed on Soviet help. Yet when the U. S. grants a loan to China, a first condition it lays down, frankly acknowledged in the press, is to alienate China from its relations with the Soviet Union. Thus the hostility of Washington against the Soviet Union, which has reached a point of hysteria during the past year, leads to the canceling out of any efforts to sustain the resistance of China to invasion.

Thus does imperialist policy always stultify and destroy every aim which, on its face, seems worthy and meritorious. Practically all Americans want their government to help China, but when such help is granted it is always given that imperialistic twist which transforms it into its opposite.

The Problem of the Spanish Refugees

There are one hundred and fifty thousand Spanish republican refugees from Franco—puppet of Hitler and Mussolini—in French concentration camps. These Spanish refugees are of deep concern to the peoples of Latin America, so much so that the Mexican Government under Cardenas, now confirmed under Camacho, opened its doors for them, and negotiated an agreement with France for their exit to come to Mexico and other Latin American countries. These facts would seem to demand from Washington some interest in the fate of the refugees, even if Washington is not moved by any humanitarian interest, even if it disregards the broad sympathy for them in the U. S., even if nothing moved it but the single selfish motive of cultivating the good will of Latin American democracy as against the Latin American reactionary circles who sympathize with Franco, Hitler and Mussolini.

But what has happened? Washington has not only refused to take a single step in behalf of the Spanish republicans, but it has obstructed and discouraged private efforts in their behalf. All those organizations, ostensibly supporting the Spanish refugees but politically affiliated to the Roosevelt Administration, have consistently done everything in their power to divert and sterilize the mass support. They repudiated the plans of the international conference in Mexico; they split the united American committee in their efforts to protect the reactionary French government from protest demonstrations against surrender of refugees to Franco; they adopted the principle: "Better that ten 'worthy' refugees be denied asylum, rather than risk that one 'hidden Communist' should be allowed to receive help."

Finally, Mrs. Roosevelt herself took the public lead in an action, described by her own supporters in *The Nation* as a "depth bomb," designed to "sink" the Rescue Ship Mission. The capitalist press took up the campaign, denouncing the Rescue Ship Mission as a "Communist plot," in the same terms Hitler and Mussolini used against the Spanish republic. When the universally venerated Helen Keller, chairman of the Rescue Ship Mission, refused to surrender to this shameful campaign, this great humanitarian—who is entirely non-political—was denounced in the public press as an "old-time agent of the Communists" in the same columns that demand outlawry and imprisonment for Communists.

What is the meaning of this public rage against the only serious effort to save the Spanish refugees? It has deep roots in Washington's foreign policy. It is the companion-piece to the hundred-million dollar loan to Franco, the fascist dictator; to curry favor with this creature of Hitler, Washington is prepared to give a slap in the face to Latin American democracy, to give joy to every fascist in the world, to affront every honest friend of the Spanish refugees in the United States.

Washington denounces "the dictators" and arms gigantically for war to "restore liberty to the entire world"; but at the same time, for the sake of slimy intrigues with bloody Franco, it indulges in these cynical crimes against the Spanish refugees. Is it any wonder that such a foreign policy proceeds from failure, to defeat, to disaster?

WASHINGTON TRIES TO "BLOW UP" THE CHILEAN POPULAR FRONT

After a long sojourn in Washington, the "Socialist" leader Senor Schnake returned to Chile just in time to throw a political "bomb" bearing the label "Made in the U.S.A." He demanded the dissolution of the Popular Front, that combination of the Radical, Socialist, and Communist parties which put the present government in power, and rescued Chile from the black reactionaries and civil war. That this effort is not successful is no fault of either Senor Schnake or the Roosevelt Administration, but is the achievement of the stern solidarity and common sense of the Chilean masses.

But consider the political significance of this disruptive effort! The United States supposedly wants stability within Chile, and the ability in that country to resist any hostile penetration. The Popular Front has given Chile such a government for the first time in years; but because it resists not only the Nazis, but also demands that the United States shall fully respect its sovereignty, Washington is exerting its full influence to break up the Popular Front, an aim which is fully shared with the circles influenced by the Nazis. Both imperialist camps are violating Chilean independence, and that they may more thoroughly come to grips with each other both want to destroy the Government which places Chilean interests above both German and United States imperialist ambitions.

But Washington and Senor Schnake are playing a very dangerous game. It is full of the same sort of inner contradictions that brought Chamberlain and Britain to grief in Europe. It will blow up in their hands, as did Chamberlain's policy, to the harm of the Chilean and the American people alike. It is a typical example of imperialist policy.

Turning Brazil into a Powder Magazine of War

Brazil furnishes another example of the explosive and catastrophic contradictions inherent in Washington's imperialist policy.

President Vargas has been a special protégé of Roosevelt. Washington encouraged and supported his bloody suppression of the great democratic mass movement, headed by the great Luis Carlos Prestes, condemned to thirty-six years' imprisonment for fighting for democracy in his country.

But Roosevelt, having helped Vargas establish and maintain his power against the masses, thereby made Vargas dependent upon the army, the landlords and the worst political reactionaries in

Brazil. And now, since Britain has been strangling Brazil with her blockade, and tries, together with Washington, to force Brazil into the war against Germany, the pro-German elements which dominate the army have countered with the demand for war against Great Britain. The Brazilian Government, having suppressed the mass movement which alone could have established a regime that, by keeping Brazil independent and neutral, would have kept the warring camps out of Brazil, now becomes a collection of foreign agents, in process of splitting apart and throwing the country into civil war to decide whether Brazil shall side with Germany or with the Anglo-American camp.

When the imperialist war enters the Americas in its aspect of military belligerency, it will in all likelihood enter through the door of Brazil, and in the form of a civil war there. This may happen in the not distant future. And when it does occur, the responsibility will rest with equal weight upon the Anglo-American imperialists and the German Nazi imperialists. For both were agreed upon the destruction of the native Brazilian democratic mass movement led by Prestes, both blessed the fantastic prison sentence to this great leader, both denied Brazil the right to independence and neutrality, and now both demand that Brazil become another pawn in the imperialist war. Their combined efforts threaten to bring upon Brazil the catastrophic role of the American "Norway."

The four examples, cited above, of the practical significance and the inner contradictions of U. S. foreign policy as applied to current problems serve to fill in the picture of just what it is that is meant when we say this war is an imperialist war, that its idealistic justifications are pure demagogy, that Washington is fully as imperialistic as Germany or Britain, and that this whole course is leading the United States to all the horrors and disasters that now afflict Europe.

It also shows concretely what we mean when we say that the inner contradictions of imperialism, which is capitalism in its stage of monopoly dominance, bring the nations into a blind alley of frustration, defeat and destruction.

It reveals, finally, in a concrete way, how imperialist policy at last creates the force which will destroy the whole system which breeds it by revealing its true criminal face to the masses of the people. It is these masses, disillusioned with the bankrupt ruling classes and their system, which will rally behind the working class for an end to the war and the class system which breeds war, and for a new system of society without oppression of man by man, of nation by nation, and, therefore, without war.

Sunday Worker, *January 19, 1941.*

VI. CRIME AGAINST CHINA

THE American loan of a hundred million dollars to China and Roosevelt's promise of much greater aid have brought the immediate result of the Kuomintang slaughter of four thousand soldiers of the New Fourth Route Army, its disbandment, and the arrest of Yeh Ting, its famous commander—a step into renewed civil war for which Chiang Kai-shek is reported to accept responsibility.

The *New York Herald Tribune* for February 1 carries a long and sober editorial on this development, which concludes:

At this juncture, when Japan is prepared to go marauding in the "South Seas" and when the Chinese should be ready, in their own interests as well as in those of their friends, to put all they have into immobilizing as big a Japanese force as possible, it is indeed a pity that they are working up a bitter domestic feud. We are confident that Chiang Kai-shek is too big to foster it; and we hope that he is big enough to bring it under control.

Yet the *Herald Tribune* writer says nothing about that which he surely knows—*why* Chiang permitted a break which he has opposed since 1938, when Kuomintang-Communist co-operation was re-established. That reason is that Chiang was given to understand that American help required him to deal with Chinese Communists as the Roosevelt Administration deals with American Communists, that American help required him to draw away from the Soviet Union and approximate Roosevelt's hostility toward that country. It is utter nonsense to speak as if this break originated in China, or with Chiang. It was pressed upon the Kuomintang from *without* as well as from within, and *from without the pressure came from Japan, Germany, England and the United States*. The ruling circles of all four powers, despite their quarrels, agreed to press upon Chiang the demand for military liquidation of the Chinese Communists.

Why It Is "Treason" to Win Victories

The Chinese Embassy in Washington on January 21 made public a cable from the Waichiaopu (Foreign Office) in Chungking, under date of January 19, giving the official explanation for the slaughter and the disbanding of the New Fourth Route Army. This is one of the most extraordinary state documents in history!

"For defiance of military orders and plot to stage a revolt" is the charge against Yeh Ting and his army. The evidence? That the Fourth Route Army, authorized at forty-five thousand men, had achieved such astounding successes that its ranks had swelled to five hundred thousand; and the Waichiaopu officially states the Government seriously considered it an *imminent danger* that Yeh Ting and his army would succeed in *"setting up a base at Nanking, Shanghai, and Hangchow, thus forming a triangular area to defy the Government."* This is all territory won, or to be won, in battle against the Japanese and their puppet regime of Wang Ching-wei. The Kuomintang armies had entirely lost this region to the Japanese and failed to regain any of it; but when the Fourth Route Army won spectacular victories for the Kuomintang government, and threatened to retake the entire area without even a minimum of help from Chunking—at that moment they are charged with mutiny and with plotting revolt, they are massacred and dispersed by their own Government!

The Kuomintang armies came into the area to smash the New Fourth Route Army in agreement and apparent collaboration with the Japanese forces. They had no collisions with the Japanese. When they had completed their first attack, they stood aside and looked on while the Japanese took up the battle to smash the Fourth Army. When the fighting was over, the Japanese and Wang

Ching-wei had regained the territory won by the valor and genius of Yeh Ting and his associates. *And the national unity of China which had held back the Japanese invaders for more than four years had been given a shattering blow!*

What the high generals of the Kuomintang could not forgive the Chinese Communists was precisely the victories won, which exposed their own consistent defeats; what above all they could not forgive was the qualities and virtues which made those victories possible, exposing the corruption and incapacity of the ruling generals.

Even the reactionary anti-Communist *Herald Tribune* must write of the Communist armies in the following terms:

A dozen correspondents and at least one competent American military observer have been behind their lines and have paid enthusiastic tribute to their splendid spirit, their amazing cleverness in getting through, between, and behind the Japanese lines at their pleasure, their good discipline and spartan mode of life and their excellent relations with the country folk, whom their agents have organized for guerrilla operations in every district the Japanese have allegedly conquered.

No one can write in such terms about armies in China, except when describing the Eighth Route and New Fourth Route armies.

But, in China, to win victories against the Japanese invaders is being interpreted as treason! That is because the capitulators, the Chinese bourgeoisie and generals have seized control again, with the understanding that Washington and London, as well as Berlin and Tokio, will back them up in delivering China again to the flames of civil war, and thus to the mercy of the Japanese invaders.

Those who do not agree should so tell Chiang Kai-shek—and the world.

Sunday Worker, *February 2, 1941.*

VII. A MONOPOLY CAPITALIST LOOKS AT THE FUTURE

I.

THE *New York Post* of January 30 gave more than a full page to the text of an address, delivered the previous evening before a scientific institute by Mr. Charles Wilson, the head of the great monopoly, General Electric.

This address was of more than ordinary interest. It was an attempt to assess the depth of the world crisis, to find its causes, and to chart a way out within the limits of capitalism. Rarely, indeed, does any spokesman for the bourgeoisie even permit such questions to be placed, not to speak of attempting to answer them. Mr. Wilson is therefore a courageous man, and what he has to say should be carefully studied.

"The world is immersed in more than a war of historically conventional character," said Mr. Wilson. "Our own beloved nation is involved in more than a temporary emergency." He calls for "recognition of the revolutionary character of this world conflict," arising from "the conflicts and confusions which have brought civilization almost to the brink of chaos."

Frankly enough, Mr. Wilson recognizes that the masses have lost faith in the capitalist system, in a paragraph worth quoting entire:

Today, the practical controlling fact is that hundreds of millions of people throughout the world have been persuaded, to the point of evangelistic conviction, that the capitalistic system is the cause of the economic insecurity of the common man and that, as the root of his economic ills, this system must be drastically modified, or failing that, destroyed.

Not so frankly, but by implication, Mr. Wilson also recognizes that the reason the masses have lost faith in capitalism is because capitalism has failed to "prove by deeds as well as by words" that it is able to meet the needs of society.

Mr. Wilson sees the present as the second stage in a world crisis that began in 1914, and which is "likely to last, with intermittent armistices of one kind or another, for two or three decades more."

He is no facile optimist. Dire forebodings for his beloved system of monopoly capital obtrude from beginning to end of a long address with the prominence of raisins liberally strewn in a rice pudding. A few samples, picked at random from the page, will convey the atmosphere he brings to us from the heights of Big Business executive circles: "dark days ahead"; "critical and confusing times"; "chaos can be the consequence of confusion and procrastination"; "world disorder"; "suspicion and condemnation"; "never before ... such a serious challenge"; "needs are so frightfully pressing"; "the coming dangerous decade"; "final stage ... most serious challenge"; "bedeviled and bewildered world"; "destructive forces flooding the world"; and so on.

How Mr. Wilson Sees Capitalism Mastering the Crisis

Despite this gloomy view of the decades ahead, Mr. Wilson bravely insists that capitalism will—must—come through and re-establish itself. He even has a program, modestly presented as a mere tentative, but a program. It looks imposing at first glance, with its division into four stages (identified as "Recovery," "Stabilization," "Backlog Building" and "Final Challenge," with eight numbered planks for the first stage, six for the second stage, five for the third stage (with four lettered sub-points) and seven for the final stage. Ah, here is the scientific mind at work, the best brains of capitalism getting down to fundamentals!

Now turn the microscope on this chart: "Recovery's needs" are listed in eight points: (1) "infinite patience" with democracy, which he sees as a drag rather than a help; (2) "respect ... the laws of our land"; (3) "free and enterprising system of free enterprise"; (4) "full-time employment of all employables"; (5) "free flow of goods...for production"; (6) "new inventions...aggressive promotion"; (7) "rural electrification...industrialization of agriculture"; (8) "hemispheric self-sufficiency...South America as a source of raw materials...subsidized."

I assure the reader that in this list I have omitted nothing except oratorical padding. These are the decisive features of Mr. Wilson's program for the first stage immediately ahead. All but three of these points are empty platitudes, or expressions of desired aims without the slightest hint of means to realize them, that is, without any "policy" at all. Point 4 on employment has meaning only in relation to armaments, which question is otherwise ignored; Point 7 is merely expression of the desire of General Electric for expansion of the rural market for its products; Point 8 is the only clear and definite policy indication, that of imperialist domination of the Americas, but even here the only hint of means to the end is "subsidy." One can only wonder how we are to pass from this first stage to the second. But taking that transition on faith, let us next try to see how Mr. Wilson will "stabilize" us.

The "stabilization stage" has only six points, as follows: (1) "credit and price control against inflation"; (2) "full supply of normal needs"; (3) "modernization of industry"; (4) "reduction of governmental activities...non-defense"; (5) "balance the non-defense budget"; (6) "industrial development of the temperate zone of South America." Here again, aside from platitudes and empty wishes, there is hardly a hint of program, except the warning that war-expenditures may be expected soon to create all the dangers of inflation, a warning canceled by Point 4.

Again we must jump to the next stage, without knowing how the transition would be made in life. We come to the "Backlog Building Stage," which is to prepare "for the days ahead, when employment connected with defense could diminish in a degree sufficient to be dangerous to our economy." That seems to indicate that this "stage" comes immediately after the war ends. The "backlogs" are (1) "further credit and term restraints" to limit consumption; (2) savings, through (a) personal, in government securities; (b) increases in unemployment insurance; (c) increases in social security payments; (d) health insurance; (3) "drastic curtailment of all governmental activities ... non-defense"; (4) "restraints on business expansion"; (5) "taxation for reduction of the national debt"; (6) "diversion of promotion expenditures to speculative promotion of pioneer products." "Here," says Mr. Wilson, "the catalog of requirements of the backlog building stage is concluded."

Here we begin to find some confusion and contradiction even in the desired aims which are expressed. Our "scientist" is not sure whether he is wishing for inflationary or deflationary influences; he is not clear whether increased governmental insurance is desired for its expanded reserves, or for its expansion of payments for immediate consumption—if for the latter, there is contradiction with other points; there is contradiction between demands for restraints on business expansion and for speculative promotion. In general, the whole conception of "backlogs" is here very confused indeed, not to mention the larger question of what role is played by this whole "stage" in the economic process.

"And now," Mr. Wilson announces with extreme gravity, "I come to the final stage—the stage when the private enterprise system will meet its most serious challenge."

This "final stage," it seems obvious, is the period of post-war crisis, although Mr. Wilson is not very clear about it, when the prop of war expenditures is taken away, when the masses are stirring and revolution is in the air everywhere, after having taken over one or more major European countries for socialism. And how is the President of General Electric, one of capitalism's most gigantic monopolies, going to lead his system to meet "its most serious challenge?" He gives the answer in his first point:

Here I submit, in all seriousness, as a first step—prayer ... as a bedeviled and bewildered world seeks the solace of Divine inspiration.

Admitting without argument that Mr. Wilson and his capitalist system will need all the Divine aid it can possibly obtain, and that

his whole program requires for its operation the miraculous intervention of Providence at every stage, we pass on to his other points:
(2) "Credit and term expansion"; (3) "More and cheaper goods";
(4) "Intensive sales promotion and advertising"; (5) "Intensification of industrial modernization"; (6) "Conversion of war plants
to consumers goods"; (7) "Permanent government public works."

Well! One can only gasp at this revelation of how the best minds
and most efficient leaders of monopoly capitalism foresee the solution of the gigantic problems piling in upon them. All the mighty
labors of this great mountain could not even bring forth a mouse,
but only this flea whose anatomy we have dissected.

Truly, these gentlemen dwell in Stygian darkness even in respect
to the structure and functioning of their own beloved system of
capitalism!

There is no need to go deeper into the analysis of Mr. Wilson's
"program," to point out how he has evaded the biggest problem of
all, namely, the war and its consequences, and the fact that the
United States is plunging into the very heart of this world struggle
for empire, bringing upon our land the full consequences of the
catastrophe. Even when he abstracts America from all this, he cannot give a coherent picture of how he would *wish* the economic
process to be directed in order to restore it to strength, without
mentioning the problem of how such a direction could be given it
in real life. He can only indulge in learned chatter, altogether
unrelated to the storms that sweep over the world of reality, to the
problems of the people.

Only the people can solve these problems, by taking their destiny
in their own hands, by taking their national economy away from
the capitalists to be operated by and for the people, through their
own state power.

We can thank Mr. Wilson for his speech, because it is such a
brilliant confirmation of the bankruptcy of capitalism, morally,
politically, physically and intellectually. The full knowledge of that
bankruptcy is the beginning of wisdom—and of revolution.

2.

Two separate and distinct approaches must be made: First, to examine the coherence of Mr. Wilson's proposals as a program, their consistency; to fix the direction in which they would lead, if any; and to relate the program to other efforts of "great thinkers" of capitalism in crisis: Second, to evaluate the program in its relation to the inherent contradictions of imperialism, its relation to the real world.

Taking up the first set of questions, we naturally want to know, in the beginning, what is Mr. Wilson's attitude toward the intervention of government in the sphere of economics. On the surface, the answer seems to be that he opposes government intervention. One of his first slogans is: "Free and enterprising system of free enterprise." Repeatedly he demands "reduction of governmental (nondefense) activities." And finally, he proposes that the capitalists shall "exercise internal self-discipline" to impose their agreed-upon program, including the decision as to how far "free enterprise" shall surrender the field to governmental "regimentation."

But among these bold words there are weasels at work. At each turn in the development of his programmatic points, he relies upon governmental intervention. And this is not in order to lead gradually toward its elimination, for, with each succeeding one of his "four stages," governmental intervention becomes more pronounced. Underlying all his proposals, there is the implicit assumption of the gigantic armaments and war program now under way. His second "stage" plumps for "price control," one of the most drastic limitations upon "free enterprise," and meaningless except it is governmental control. His third "stage" relies upon expansion of governmental expenditures on social security measures. Finally, his fourth "stage" comes to a climax with "permanent government public works." It is clear, that if Mr. Wilson is a "free enterprise" champion, he is also a defeatist, who has already reconciled himself to a governmental straitjacket as being indispensable to hold the disintegrating capitalist system together.

The result of this is that Mr. Wilson is of two minds. He demands "drastic curtailment" of governmental intervention, and in the same breath himself proposes most far-reaching interventions which grow in scope and permanency. He cannot make up his mind to go consistently in either direction. Unable to plant himself firmly on either stool, he falls between them.

Mr. Wilson is equally bifurcated in his thinking about inflation. He tacitly accepts inflation tendencies, arising from huge armaments and war expenditures, as the motive force of "recovery," his first stage. His second stage begins with a warning of inflation, against which "credit and price control" must be used. In the fourth stage of development of his policy, he is back again relying upon inflation, expressed in "credit and term expansion."

Perhaps this vacillation between inflationary and deflationary proposals is explained by the desire at one point to stimulate economic activity, and at the other point to hold it back, expedients to "level out" the business cycle? If so intended, however, the inner contradictions of the program only become sharper, for along with deflationary policies he increases his emphasis on expansionist measures, at home ("modernization of industry," "speculative promotion of pioneer products"), and abroad ("industrial development of . . . South America"), which indeed run through his *four* stages.

Is this apparent contradiction reconciled by making expansion at one time in production goods, and at the other time in consumption goods—is it explained as measures to limit consumption in favor of capital (or war) expenditures, and then (with war ending) the expansion of consumers goods to take up the slack of the failing war market? No, this is not the answer; strangely enough, we find Mr. Wilson demanding in his "second stage" (clearly war time), "full supply of normal needs . . . to all strata of society," while in his next stage (clearly that of transition to peace, the ending of war), he emphasizes instead "restraints" to limit consumption, and brings forward expansion of social insurance, not as a means of distributing purchasing power among the masses, but under the head of "savings," as a "socially desirable form of accumulation," as a means of postponing consumption.

Enough has been revealed, even in this brief examination of Mr. Wilson's economic program, to establish that it is not possessed of inner consistency, that it is incoherent, that it does not point any clear direction of economic policy.

But there is a clear political direction woven into the incoherent economic platform. There is the sharp demand that monopoly capital's private property in the nation's economy shall not be infringed upon. Behind the bland promises of "infinite patience" with democracy, and "respect for the laws of the land," lies the implied threat of an opposite attitude toward any "democracy" and "law" which dares to attack or infringe upon that private property. The demand for "free enterprise" is in reality the demand for freedom of monopoly to crush out small enterprise. The political direction of Mr. Wilson is definitely toward fascism or Nazism for America.

With Mr. Wilson, the monopoly executive, the "economic program" is only the trimmings, the "learned chatter," with which to cover up the fascist political policy. For a clear statement of the economic policy of American fascism, one can much better turn to Herbert Hoover's speech last year at the University of Pennsylvania, or the deeds, contrasted with the words, of Roosevelt. The connecting link between the Wilson and Hoover "programs" is their common demand for "South America as a source of raw materials." It is the concept of the new world empire, which Dr. Virgil Jordan developed with such richness last December before the Investment Bankers Association.

The "Program" vs. the Real World

It remains to measure Mr. Wilson's program with the current realities of the world in which it must be applied. That world is a world at war, a war of unexampled destructiveness, a war brought on by the inherent weaknesses, failures and contradictions of the self-same capitalist system (in its monopoly stage), a war which Mr. Wilson relies upon to deliver us out of the crisis.

Mr. Wilson's program has some very good points. For example, "Rural electrification and industrialization of agriculture." It is an essential step, upon which human progress depends. If the capitalist system could bring this about, this one thing would guarantee it another lease on life.

But monopoly capital cannot carry out this "good point" without turning it into a new source of misery for the masses and a new basis for crisis. That is the trouble with all of Mr. Wilson's proposals. As long as monopoly capital and private property are in the saddle, the "industrialization of agriculture" could only mean the creation of new giant capitalist farms, the ruin and expropriation of the small owners, and the transformation of the whole farming population into a rural proletariat. That is the inner contradiction, the inherent fatal disease of capitalism in its monopoly stage.

In actual reality, capitalism, that system of "free enterprise," has held back agriculture from participation in technical advancement, except in stunted and fragmentary form; capitalism had plunged agriculture into a chronic crisis for years before the industrial crisis broke over the capitalist world. Exactly the same formula of "free enterprise," which stunted agriculture and brought crisis, is offered as the cure of crisis. But not the slightest reason is, or can be, brought forward to support the belief that the hair of the dog will cure his bite.

Similarly with that most admirable objective: "Full-time employment of all employables." If the capitalist system could achieve that end, in any other form than compulsory labor in a military state, then it would indeed still have some life in it yet; we could not envisage its quick disappearance. But in Mr. Wilson's program, and in that of all ideologists of capitalism, such phrases as "full employment" are empty demagogy. Capitalism requires the army of the unemployed, and in its monopoly stage it builds that army up to gigantic proportions.

There is only one country that has achieved full-time employment of all employables, and that is the Union of Soviet Socialist Republics.

The course of economic development in the United States shows that the highest productivity of labor corresponds to the greatest unemployment. That is the *reality* of America today, and it is inseparably connected with the very nature of capitalism; for, as capital increases, with the rise in the productivity of labor, it increases the part that is spent on machinery, raw materials, etc., and decreases the part that is spent on labor. In a word, as long as the economy of the country remains the private property of a handful of Mr. Wilsons, every advance in technique is made by throwing additional working people out to starve. Mr. Wilson cannot have monopoly capital and enduring economic stability at the same time.

Perhaps the best example of the impossibility of reconciling monopoly capital with social progress is the fate of new inventions under monopoly. The material progress of society depends upon the unrestricted development of science and invention; and Mr. Wilson, unable to ignore this, tips his hat to it in his proposals. But here again, *reality* shows that it is precisely monopoly capital that stands in the way of the unrestricted use of scientific inventions. Only a society based on production for use by the people and not for the profit of a handful of monopolists will permit the free, creative use of science and invention. Every study of this question that has been made in America in recent years bears this out. One of these studies entitled *Industrial Research and Changing Technology,* a W.P.A. National Research Project, shows that industrial research is controlled by the big trusts, with the result that about one hundred and fifty thousand industrial corporations that required organized research activities were without research laboratories, not to speak of the large number of unincorporated enterprises. This monopoly of research enables monopoly capital to use it to increase its own profits before anything else. As this study puts it:

The business policies which influence the course of research are directed primarily toward assuring the continued security and profitability of the existing investments. The flow of industrially applicable discoveries is therefore channeled to a considerable extent within the requirements of a comparatively small number of concerns.

Mr. Wilson's own industry provides a sufficiently striking example of this very process, as the following passage indicates from one of the studies by the National Resources Committee:

Changes within the electric industry have been retarded by the buying and suppressing of patents by the large corporations which dominate the field. From 1896 to 1911 the General Electric and the Westinghouse electric companies had a patent-purchasing agreement that neither would acquire a patent that would tend to injure the other, and many inventors could not find a market for their patents. A superior electric lamp, which it is estimated will save electric light users $10,000,000 a year, has been invented but has not been put on the market.

In other words, the real hopelessness of Mr. Wilson's "program" is revealed precisely by his most important proposals, those affecting the foundations of the capitalist system, namely, the question of the employment of all employables, the question of industrial and scientific progress, the question of the status of the overwhelming majority of propertyless masses. Mr. Wilson's entire "program" is predicated on the existence of monopoly capital, but unfortuately for Mr. Wilson, monopoly capital means decaying, dying capitalism which no "cure" can save.

The capitalist world is busily engaged in fratricidal war, the nations are exerting superhuman efforts to destroy one another. The net result is the destruction of the very foundations of the capitalist system. It is impossible for capitalism to be restored. The world must sink into chaos, or go forward to socialism, the common ownership and operation of the national economy by all the people. The guarantee that the world will rise out of chaos, will achieve socialism, lies in the fact that the masses see before their eyes, not only the debacle of capitalism, but also the unexampled success of socialism, as the most practical and prosperous—as the only practical and prosperous—way to peace and human progress.

Sunday Worker, *February 9 and 16, 1941.*

VIII. THE AMERICAN SPIRIT

THE spirit of America was invoked in strident tones by the third inaugural address of President Roosevelt. But the spirit which obviously moved the President's address revealed no resemblance to the spirit of America.

The spirit in which great Americans have traditionally addressed the people on great occasions was uniformly a spirit of *modesty*. I cite a few examples:

> Not unconscious in the outset of the inferiority of my qualifications, experience, in my own eyes—perhaps still more in the eyes of others— has strengthened the motives to diffidence in myself....
>
> —George Washington, Farewell Address, Sept. 17, 1796.

> A diffidence, perhaps too just, in my own qualification, will teach me to look with reverence to the examples of public virtue left by my illustrious predecessors, and with veneration to the lights that flowed from the mind that founded and the mind that reformed our system. The same diffidence induces me to hope for instruction and aid from the co-ordinate branches of the government....
>
> —Andrew Jackson, Inaugural, March 4, 1829.

Lincoln's public life was so uniformly an expression of this characteristic modesty that any particular quotation from his utterances would be supererogation.

Roosevelt strikes a new and coarse note—one of vainglory and boasting. "We acted, we acted quickly, boldly, decisively," he says in description of his own role. And in conclusion he explains that he remains President "by the will of God!" Most American Presidents have invoked Divine assistance, but Roosevelt is the first to claim Divine "sanction" since the "Divine right of kings" was abolished by the Revolution proclaimed in the Declaration of Independence.

"The co-ordinate branches of the government continue freely to function," Roosevelt declared, while admitting the dire crisis in the world and "at home." But he did not mention his usurpation of September 3, 1940, when he seized power to dispose of warships to a foreign belligerent power and to negotiate war alliances, nor did he quote Jefferson's words which warned against such usurpations:

It would be perfidious ... not to warn you of encroachments, which, though clothed with the pretext of necessity, or disguised by arguments of expediency, may yet establish precedents, which may ultimately devote a generous and unsuspicious people to all the consequences of usurped power. . . . Exhortations to disregard domestic usurpations until foreign danger shall have passed is an artifice which may be forever used; because the possessors of power, who are the advocates for its extension, can ever create national embarrassments, to be successively employed to soothe the people into sleep, whilst that power is swelling silently, secretly, and fatally. Of the same character are insinuations of a foreign influence, which seize upon a laudable enthusiasm against danger from abroad, and distort it by an unnatural application, so as to blind your eyes against danger at home.

"The Bill of Rights remains inviolate," Roosevelt said. By thus denying violations he expressed his approval of the rising wave of repressions and limitations on popular rights, which he personally initiated, denying the validity of the Bill of Rights to those who suffer these repressions. He did not mention the Alien Registration Law, for which he bears personal responsibility, and its accompanying modern versions of the Alien and Sedition Law of 1798; nor did he quote the famous Virginia resolutions, and "Address to the People," cornerstones of American democracy, in "protest against the palpable and alarming infractions of the Constitution, in the two late cases of the 'Alien and Sedition Acts.' . . . If a suspicion that aliens are dangerous constitute the justification of that power exercised over them by Congress, then a similar suspicion will justify the exercise of a similar power over natives. . . . Let the artificers of monarchy be asked what farther materials they can need for building up their favorite system."

"The freedom of elections is wholly maintained," Roosevelt declared. But at that moment he was celebrating the victory of the most gigantic rigging ever put over in the name of an election. The most important new converts to Roosevelt, the "economic royalists," had ganged up on the Republican Party Convention, which they normally control, and forced it to nominate a Democrat, Wendell Willkie, who had specifically engaged himself to stand on the same foreign-policy platform as Roosevelt. Both Willkie and Roosevelt promised the voters peace, in their pre-election speeches, and both agreed to forget the promise after election. To make sure this rigged election would not bring a revolt of the voters, the only party that offered a genuine alternative, the Communist Party, was forcibly and illegally removed from the ballot in the most important states, its candidates and election workers sentenced to prison in other states (one candidate to fifteen years), an official Red hunt instituted everywhere to drive Communists and their supporters out of public or private employment—and Mr. Roosevelt boasts in his inaugural address: "The freedom of elections is wholly maintained." Thomas Jefferson described this sort of election-jobber, in 1795:

These rogues set out with stealing the people's good opinion, and then steal from them the right of withdrawing it, by contriving laws and associations against the power of the people themselves.

Roosevelt's whole program is predicated upon the assumption that the British navy is the "first line of defense" for the American people. He would like to have forgotten the words of Jefferson, which read as if they were written for today in repudiation of Roosevelt. Read this from Jefferson:

We should first let England plunder us, says Jefferson, explaining the policy of Anglophile Americans, as she has been doing for years, for fear Bonaparte should do it; and then ally ourselves with her, and enter into the war. . . . And, what is to be our security, that when embarked for her in the war, she will . . . not leave us in the lurch? Her good faith! The faith of a nation of merchants! The *Punica fides* of modern Carthage! Of the friend and protectress of Copenhagen! [One year before this was written, Britain had bombarded Copenhagen and captured the Danish fleet, without warning, under pretext of "protection."] Of the nation who never admitted a chapter of morality into her political code! And is boldly avowing that whatever power can make hers, is hers of right. Money, and not morality, is the principle of commerce and commercial nations. But in addition to this, the nature of the English government forbids, of itself, reliance on her engagements; and it is well known that she had been the least faithful to her alliances of any nation of Europe, since the period of her history wherein she has been distinguished for her commerce and corruption. (1810.)

Jefferson wrote this description of the British role at Munich, one hundred and twenty-eight years before the event.

To complete and universalize the desolation of the globe, it has been the will of Providence to raise up, at the same time, a tyrant as unprincipled and as overwhelming, for the ocean. Not in the poor maniac George, but in his government and nation. Bonaparte will die, and his tyrannies with him. But a nation never dies. The English government, and its piratical principles and practices, have no fixed term of duration. Europe feels, and is writhing under the scorpion whips of Bonaparte. We are assailed by those of England. . . . The object of England is the *permanent domination of the ocean,* and the *monopoly of the trade of the world.* (1813.)

This was written when the British were engaged in sacking Washington and burning the White House, and the Capitol.

Roosevelt is engaged in a gigantic effort to replace this long-standing American tradition with its direct opposite, which is most completely expressed in the semi-official agitation for "union now" with the British empire. That is doubtless why he has publicly rebuked the memory of Jefferson, and paid homage to that of Hamilton. Doubtless also that is why the Democratic Party suddenly ceased to observe Jackson Day Today's "Anglomen," as Jefferson called the Hamiltonian party of his time, have of course advanced greatly beyond their predecessors; they dream that in the new Anglo-American world empire, Wall Street will be "the center of gravity," and that "the scepter passes to the United States." Therefore, Jefferson's excoriation of the British "pirates" must now be enlarged to include the Wall Street "pirates."

Roosevelt's policies represent the imperialist denial of the people's right and will to live. His deepest and most subtle violation of the American tradition, the American spirit, in his inaugural address occurs therefore when he seemingly pledges himself to "democracy" most emphatically. Consider the following:

The life of a nation is the fullness of the measure of its will to live. . . . There are men who believe that democracy . . . is limited or measured by a kind of mystical or artificial fate—that, for some unexplained reason, tyranny and slavery have become the surging wave of the future, and that freedom is an ebbing tide. But we Americans know that this is not true.

Yet the best representatives of the American spirit never told our people that the "will to live" of a ruling class (its will to grow richer) would solve the problems of or avoid the dangers to democracy—that is, the masses, the people. The best Americans never tired of warning that democracy, regardless of its "will to live," could not endure unless the masses maintained the possibilities of struggle against minority ruling classes, unless its material preconditions were maintained; they saw democracy's "fate" dependent upon the material factors and political power in the masses, without which freedom would become "an ebbing tide," overwhelmed by the "surging wave" of tyranny and slavery.

Turn to Lincoln: in his Presidential message to the first regular session of Congress (December, 1861), Lincoln fixed precisely the material preconditions for the democracy of his day, without which no "will to live" could be of any avail, in the following words:

Men with their families—wives, sons, daughters—work for themselves on their farms, in their houses, and in their shops, taking the whole product to themselves, and asking no favors of capital on the one hand, nor of hired laborers or slaves on the other.

Unless the great body of the population occupies this independent economic position—depending neither upon capital nor hired labor, Lincoln foresaw that *"all of liberty shall be lost."*

In this Lincoln was but expounding the doctrines of Thomas Jefferson, who foresaw and warned against the rising institution of combined great wealth and political power, such as Roosevelt's war program represents today, and—

Though the day may be at some distance ... yet it will surely come, when a single fibre of this institution will produce an hereditary aristocracy, which will change the form of our government from the best to the worst in the world. (Letter to Washington, 1786.)

Roosevelt now ignores and hides the most important facts (which he temporarily utilized himself in 1937 in his fight against the Supreme Court). These are:

That the material foundations of Jeffersonian-Lincolnian democracy have been irretrievably lost;

That power-driven machinery has destroyed forever the individual private-property basis for democracy, and transformed the national economy into private property *against democracy,* in the hands of a "hereditary aristocracy" built of wealth and political power;

That there is no way to restore democracy to a solid foundation, except to make the national economy, instead of the sacrifices of war, "a common enterprise" in the hands of the "common people" —which is socialism, the only possible path forward;

When all these things are ignored, hidden, or even denied, as they are by Roosevelt, and substituted by the bare "will to live," which is really only the "will to empire" of the economic royalists, then *the net result is treason to democracy, and violation of the American spirit.*

In truth, Roosevelt is consciously striving to become the great American imperialist leader on the grand scale. This imperialist role is the antithesis of the living heart of the American tradition. Just as bourgeois historians are rewriting American history to glorify Benedict Arnold, Aaron Burr, and General Conway, to replace Washington, Jefferson, Paine; just as bourgeois novelists bring out an *Oliver Wiswell* to embellish treason and spatter mud on the American Revolution; just as bourgeois motion picture magnates produce *Gone With the Wind* and *Santa Fé Trail* to idealize the slave society and drag down the popular understanding of the high character and historically progressive significance of a Lincoln and a John Brown—so does Franklin D. Roosevelt perform a similar part on the American political stage.

Roosevelt represents the negation of the traditional American spirit, as surely and as completely as American imperialism with its fevered ambitions of world empire is the negation of everything represented by Washington, Jefferson, Jackson and Lincoln.

New Masses, *February 18, 1941.*

IX. THE GREAT TRADITION

I AM very happy to join with you in the celebration of the thirtieth anniversary of this great institution, the *New Masses*. I should really have been permitted to be a listener this afternoon, not a talker. One should not speak at such an important occasion, at such a great gathering without adequate preparation. I came here without that necessary preparation. I will therefore speak quite at random and extemporaneously. My remarks will largely be my spontaneous reactions to the magnificent program given to us here this afternoon and that magnificent anniversary edition of the *New Masses* issued this week.

As I sat here this afternoon, I asked myself the question: What is it that makes these meetings distinctive, something that could not be reproduced by any other group of people in America? What is it that brings this audience, the readers of the *New Masses,* together and makes this institution live, although according to the prevailing standards of our society, it should be a financially bankrupt institution, tottering on the edge of the abyss every moment of existence? What is it that brings you supporters of this paper together and enables this magazine to surmount every crisis—and it has a crisis on the average of twice a week? What is it that makes one proud to think to himself: I helped save the *New Masses?* And there are tens of thousands of us and we are all congratulating ourselves at one time or other that each of us has saved the *New Masses.*

We are a unique group; we are searching for truth, and that binds us together with a bond that transcends most ordinary bonds, that gives us a power to do things that ordinary aggregations of humanity cannot do, and out of this fellowship that has been built up over the years and grows stronger and stronger, we have created an institution in which we are collectively not only the direct producers of the magizine, but its readers, a great broad grouping that is identified with this institution. We have created that atmosphere, or, better still, we have fertilized the American soil out of which has been able to grow most of the living manifestations of American culture today.

It is not an accident that even the decrepit and decaying American bourgeoisie, in order to conduct its struggle against us, has to borrow its weapons from our arsenal. It is no accident that the Republican National Convention, in order to make any kind of a cultural face, had to put on Earl Robinson's *Ballad for Americans*. That is typical, and even if they want to produce a great best-seller for the bourgeoisie, they have to resort to someone who had sneaked into our midst and had been kicked out. This great best seller of the day—what is the name of it—"Out of the Sewer"?— that is a symbol of the culture of the American bourgeoisie today, a real symbol that stands for the cultural level to which the rulers of this country have descended. The whole machinery of the great American society, the most powerful nation in the world, is put to work to spread that book over the face of America.

We have our best seller. Our best seller this year is the Dean of Canterbury. That is a symbol of the cultural life that we are bringing to America. Let the two camps be judged by their best sellers —capitalism, with its "Out of the Sewer"; socialism, with the Dean of Canterbury's *The Soviet Power*.

These contrasts run throughout every phase of life. We have already registered in various publications in the past period the development of this profoundly reactionary current in American history and literature, the bourgeois revaluation of its own past and its repudiation of its own past. Years ago when we first began to speak in clear and definite tones in our claim as the inheritors of the American revolutionary tradition, as the modern representatives of Washington, Jefferson, Paine and Lincoln, some people thought that this was merely a sort of protective coloration put on by those terrible Reds who wanted to tear down this American tradition and, in order to do it, hid themselves in a Trojan Horse and disguised themselves as advocates of the American tradition. If anyone has any lingering suspicion of that any more, just let him look around at what the thinkers, writers, spokesmen and ideologists of our ruling class are doing and saying today. The most significant history that they brought out in this past period was the debunking of Washington and the raising of General Conway to the position of the misunderstood genius of the American Revolution; Conway of the notorious Conway cabal! One of the most serious historical studies they have brought forward has been the belated recognition of Benedict Arnold and his restoration to the galaxy of American heroes! One of the most significant efforts which is gaining great recognition and influence in our history circles is to restore Aaron Burr as a model for the youth of today!

The greatest literary effort of the bourgeoisie in the past period has been *Gone With the Wind,* a "great effort," eighty years after the Civil War, to refurbish the glories of a slave society and to drag down the great tradition of Lincoln and the emancipation struggle. One of the current efforts of the great movie trust is the "epic" picture *Sante Fé Trail,* built upon the thesis that the great John Brown was a dirty little Red, a fanatic advocating force and violence, an enemy of society, of all that is good and gracious in culture; the thesis that the representatives of human dignity, decency and culture of that day are not John Brown or Abraham Lincoln, but the flowers of the slave system. The great general is Robert E. Lee, in charge of the hanging of John Brown. I don't know why they did not also bring in one of his assistants at that hanging, John Wilkes Booth, who is unquestionably also one of the heroes that they still keep in the closet and who will be revealed to us in the second dispensation of the new culture that the bourgeoisie is giving to America today.

As in all of these other things, so in our political life we are being given one of the most profoundly reactionary regimes that not only America but the world has ever seen, covered with the tawdry trappings of a cheaply bought progressive reputation. American politics today are so completely reactionary, corrupt and degenerate that even Burton K. Wheeler, who four years ago was the leader of the reactionary camp in the fight around the Supreme Court, stands out in that swamp in Washington as a sort of progressive giant.

The only voice, clear and uncompromising, that we hear in the official circles of America is the lone American Labor Congressman, Vito Marcantonio.

A great wave of reaction has engulfed America. In appearance it is overwhelmingly strong, and we are a puny handful who stand up and brave the lightning of their storms, apparently doomed to utter annihilation. That is the appearance. But behind this surface appearance the reality is something else. This great gathering of the forces of reaction, this unlimited offensive against everything that is honest and decent in American life is a sign not of the strength of reaction in America; it is a sign that the whole ruling class today is becoming conscious of its own doom. It is a sign that the American bourgeoisie has read its own death warrant and is in a hysterical fit of resistance to the inevitable. And we, though small in numbers today—and the future always first presents itself not with the majority but with a small minority—we represent the future of America. We represent the American search for truth; we represent the American tradition of democracy, of government of, by and for the people. We represent honest thought and culture; we represent the search for beauty; we represent the creative power of the masses. And that is why the future belongs to us. If the bourgeoisie still dreams that in America they can continue their bankrupt and decrepit system by adopting the new technique of Adolph Hitler, let them take a second thought. That is a false hope. They did not begin the job quickly enough. Already there is such a growing opinion, knowledge, culture, understanding, intellectual power in the masses of America that the most powerful reactionary regime can never cut it out.

In 1939 we already had a best seller, a great book, the *History of the Communist Party of the Soviet Union.* Close to two hundred thousand copies of that book were sold. No American Hitler will ever be able to cut out of American society the seeds that were sown with the distribution and the study and the reading of that book in every nook and corner of America. That lesson has been absorbed deep into the consciousness and the subconsciousness and the blood and bones of America. And now there has been sold the first quarter of a million of the Dean of Canterbury's great book, *The Soviet Power,* which is not a Communist book, by the way—indicating that people don't have to be Communists to come to us any more; all they have to be is honest and decent and they have no other place to go. And when as against this great instrument the bourgeoisie is able to put up only such puny weapons, it is really a pitiful spectacle. They have completely departed from everything that was once great in their tradition. They are corpses, socially and politically speaking, waiting for an aroused and organized working class to bury them and remove the stench that now poisons the atmosphere of our country.

The *New Masses* represents this great creative movement of the people in its broadest aspects. Therefore we know that the thirtieth anniversary of the *New Masses* is not going to be the last. The *New Masses* will go ahead; it will move forward in the forefront of this great gathering movement of the people, and the banner of the *New Masses* will be standing at the celebration of the final victory of the people over all exploiters and oppressors, and that will not be in the next thirty years of the *New Masses.* History is traveling fast now. Thirty years ago we did not have the radio and the airplane; today we have them and many other factors speeding up the process of history, and the minds of men are speeding up.

Millions of Americans are already absorbing the lessons of the new society, understanding that the old has nothing but death and destruction for them; they are beginning to see the flower of the new and its tremendous promise for our land, and we will realize that promise because this generation and the masses of America are going to bring our America to the flowering of socialism.

Speech delivered at the thirtieth anniversary celebration of the New Masses, *February 16, 1941.*

X. THE FINAL VERDICT WILL BE WRITTEN BY THE PEOPLE

I WANT TO apologize for coming here unprepared to make a speech. I have been busy the last few days getting ready to go away to camp. My number came up and so I am having something like the experience of millions of Americans today. Practically every home in America is waiting to see when the number is coming up that takes away one or more members of the family. All America is going through this experience. It is true that the other boys are being told they are going for one year, but just the other day one of the higher ranking generals of the United States Army told a gathering of conscripts in one of the camps: "Forget about that nonsense of one year; you are in for the duration." And that is the decision of the representatives of the American ruling class down in Washington. They have taken us in "for the duration."

I am over the draft age, so they had to find a special reason for drafting me and our good friend and comrade William Wiener, and they found special reasons for drafting quite a few more. But these reasons are of the same validity and the same character of which every fascist dictatorship has proceeded to silence the opposition.

They say that I am going because I committed a crime. It is true that it was many years ago, and it did not injure anybody. I only used some names to which I was not legally entitled in order to get certain rights of travel to which I was entitled—a technical question, no harm to anybody involved. But by fine-spun legal sophistry which has been endorsed by the Supreme Court, this whole technical business, which even Herbert Hoover had discarded, was dug out of the pigeonholes by the Roosevelt Administration as a convenient pretext for giving the signal for a general all-around offensive against the rights and liberties and well being and peace of the whole American people. They say I used a fraudulent passport. It happens that the passport was in my own name and merely secured me entry into the United States to which I was completely entitled with or without a passport. Nobody was deceived, nobody injured.

But there are some false passports which do great injury. I was just recalling a while ago that there is an old song that used to be very popular in America from that Gilbert and Sullivan opera—I think it is *The Mikado*—where the Lord High Executioner sings about making the punishment fit the crime. If my kind of crime rates four years in prison, I wonder what should be the punishment for a man who got a false passport by deceiving the whole American people? I refer to Franklin D. Roosevelt, who got his passport for a third term by promising to keep America out of this imperialist war, and then violating that promise.

If my passport offense rates four years, what is the punishment that fits the crime of Franklin D. Roosevelt against the American people? I think the punishment that will inevitably be inflicted for that crime—the supreme punishment—will be written by history, which will write down that name as the man who betrayed the peace and prosperity of the American people.

They used to say in the old days—how long ago it seems—when the Administration was bucking the economic royalists in America, that Mr. Roosevelt was a traitor to his class. Well, now the prodigal has returned. He has gone back to his class. The fatted calf was killed in honor of his return. Some millions of American boys are going to be thrown into the sacrifice to make it a real celebration, and today he truly represents his class.

But it is a class which has long outlived its role in history. It has nothing more to contribute except war, conscription, dictatorship, destruction of the rights and livelihood of the people, catastrophe, famine, pestilence and chaos, which are spreading rapidly over the face of the earth and drawing ever closer to our own shores.

THE FUTURE BELONGS TO THE PEOPLE

We are not overwhelmed by this prospect, however. The forces of war and reaction seem to be overwhelmingly strong and we who stand out against it seem to be quite a small minority group. But we are not dismayed by this. Strange as it may seem, to those who see only the surface of events, it is not we of this small minority who lie awake at nights. I sleep quite soundly myself. I have the impression that most Communists sleep quite soundly at night. And yet I hear that there is a great epidemic of insomnia among the bourgeoisie.

Down in Washington bed clothes are being torn by fat bodies tossing around. Perhaps you think the conscience of these gentlemen is troubling them. Here and there, there is a vestige of conscience playing its part. However, most of them got rid of their conscience long ago.

The thing that keeps them awake, the thing that denies them rest is that they have been trying to look into the future. They gaze into their crystal ball and, try as they will, they cannot figure out where the world is going to. They cannot see any future except the intensification of starvation, war, pestilence, destruction, chaos. They hire their scribblers, their Norman Thomases to soothe the people with stories of the beautiful world that is going to come after the war, but they bought that stuff so they don't believe it themselves.

They can see no future and they know that the day of reckoning is coming. They know that the people will not forever remain patient; they know that for all their great powers they are completely helpless in the face of the sweep of events. They are even beginning to realize that the more energetically they carry out their policies, the more surely they come to collapse. They are beginning to realize that their trouble is some fatal internal contradictions. They can no more escape from them than a man can lift himself by his boot-straps. And they realize that the people are beginning to understand that the only way out of this bloody mess that imperialism is creating in the world is the way out of capitalism, the way to a new, socialist world.

The majority of the American people do not understand socialism; they do not as yet understand that war and capitalism are inseparable. We still have to teach them that, but we have powerful aids in this teaching today. The government in Washington is helping us to teach the American people this way out. The whole capitalist press is helping us to teach the people this great lesson today. In spite of the fact that the newspapers are filled from beginning to end with lies designed to hide this great truth, it emerges clearer and clearer even in the pages of the capitalist press.

We face the future with great confidence. The future always presents itself as a small minority. It is only with the development of a great historic crisis that new majorities come into being and new courses are taken by history. Not every minority becomes a majority and it is not because we are a minority that we are the representatives of the future. I could name you plenty of minorities that have very little chance in the future. But we have very solid reasons for believing that we are the minority that represents the future.

It is first of all because we are that minority which is working, fighting, organizing to achieve what the overwhelming majority of the American people want—to get out and stay out of the imperialist war. And also another solid reason is our calm confidence in the future, that we represent that party and that program which is already realizing that future in the socialist one-sixth of the earth, the Soviet Union.

But here in the midst of a world where the great powers, the great aggregation of the political leadership of the human race, the great aggregation of wealth, the great institutions of science and learning, the churches, the movies, the newspapers, the radio, the armies, the navies, and the air fleets are all mobilized for destruction, killing, bombing, machine-gunning, torpedoing, blowing the world to bits, throwing whole continents into pestilence and death—all they can say to their own people is: fight on to victory. And victory means beginning the cycle all over again. In the midst of that, here is a great country, one-sixth of the world, which, despite the most elaborate conspiracy and provocation that history has ever seen, has managed to keep itself out of this bloody chaos, has already managed to rescue 23,000,000 of its most immediate neighbors.

THE SOVIET UNION

While the destruction goes on in the rest of the world the Soviet Union is building its new economy at a rate never witnessed before in history, and it keeps up this rate in the midst of a world at war. At the recent Conference of the Communist Party, they began to elaborate a new stage in the development of that new society; they began to draw up a fifteen-year plan. They are now finishing the Third Five-Year Plan. That of the next fifteen years is going to be a plan made in one piece, and in those fifteen years, the Soviet Union is going to overtake and surpass, economically as well as in every other respect, every other country in the world, including the United States.

Of course, we have heard of plans and plans and plans, and to speak of a plan in most cases means to speak of some empty promise, like Roosevelt's fraudulent promise to keep America out of this war. But through three Five-Year Plans in the Soviet Union we have learned to expect the plans not only to be fulfilled; the plans are overfulfilled.

We are not yet in a position to do for our country what the Communists have been able to do for the great territories of the Soviet Union. The same sort of program for America would bring much quicker and greater results because in this country we already have the material pre-conditions for socialism, the material conditions that they can create only over long years and with painful effort, there. Here, these conditions were created by capitalism before it grew old and senile and died on its feet and began to stink.

Once the American people take control of their own destiny, take control of their own country, take control of their own economy and eliminate these war-making parasites who strangle our country economically, who corrupt it culturally and politically, and who now threaten to destroy it in the imperialist war—once we get rid of these parasites, America can over night be transformed into a garden of prosperity and security and peace.

We know that the American people will not forever and not for long submit to this kind of system and this kind of leadership. Our own ruling class can launch us into this war but they cannot end it. The American pepole can end it; the American people will end it, and the American people will find the way to this all the quicker because the American people have produced already a Communist Party, a party with roots among the masses, a party that can never be separated from the American masses, a party that will always be at work amongst the American masses, a party that will organize and lead the American people to peace and to socialism.

Speech delivered at Mecca Temple, New York, February 24, 1941. This was one of four protest meetings held in New York on February 24, at which Earl Browder spoke. Similar "Free Browder" rallies were held throughout the United States.

INDEX